# Fresh Paint!

# Fresh Paint!

## New Looks for Unfinished Furniture

### 45 FUN AND FESTIVE PROJECTS

Jane LaFerla

LARK BOOKS

A Division of Sterling Publishing Co., Inc.
New York

Art Director: Celia Naranjo
Art Assistant: Hannes Charen
Photographer: Evan Bracken

Library of Congress Cataloging-in-Publication Data
LaFerla, Jane.
    Fresh paint! : new looks for unfinished furniture : 45 fun and festive
projects / Jane LaFerla. — 1st ed.
        p. cm/
    Includes index.
    ISBN 1-57990-260-X
    1. Furniture painting. 2. Decoration and ornament. I. Title.
TT199.4.L34  1999
    684.1—dc21                                                98-39947
                                                               CIP

10 9 8 7 6 5 4 3 2 1

Published by Lark Books, a division of
Sterling Publishing Co., Inc.
387 Park Avenue South, New York, N.Y. 10016

 1999 Lark Books

Distributed in Canada by Sterling Publishing,
c/o Canadian Manda Group, One Atlantic Ave., Suite 105
Toronto, Ontario, Canada M6K 3E7

Distributed in Australia by Capricorn Link (Australia) Pty Ltd., P.O.
Box 6651, Baulkham Hills, Business Centre
NSW 2153, Australia

Distributed in the U.K. by:
Guild of Master Craftsman Publications Ltd.
Castle Place 166 High Street, Lewes, East Sussex, England, BN7 1XU
Tel: (+ 44) 1273 477374  Fax: (+ 44) 1273 478606
Email: pubs@thegmcgroup.com, Web: www.gmcpublications.com

If you have questions or comments about this book, please contact:
Lark Books
50 College St.
Asheville, NC 28801
(828) 253-0467

Printed in China.

ISBN 1-57990-260-X

# Contents

# Buy It!
# Paint It!
# Love It!

**W**hy settle for furniture that looks like you bought it any-where, when you can have fun creating your own unique looks with unfinished furniture? In a few hours, you can transform a plain piece into a useful work of art that is as enjoyable to make as it is to own.

Don't worry about learning painstaking techniques. With unfinished furniture, you can get right to the fun stuff. By starting with clean, bare wood, you eliminate the added mess of stripping off years of old finishes. So forget about knowing stains from grains, just pick up your brush and go.

The best part is that only you will know what you paid for it—most of the pieces in this book cost less than two dinners out plus tickets to a movie.

## Old Ways, New Looks

The concept of painted furniture extends back through the ages. As one of the easiest ways to introduce pattern and color to an interior, painted furniture has evolved in one form or another through many of the world's cultures. Even without a formal course in art history, most of us can at least conjure vague images of Chinese lacquer work, Scandinavian folk-art designs, and Pennsylvania Dutch and German motifs.

Now, with the recent explosion of interest in decorative painting, and the easily accessible information that's avail-able about it, once paint-phobic people have been inspired to color their walls, floors, and furniture using traditional techniques.

A renewed interest in bright interior colors, combined with the emphasis on finding an expressive personal style, has liberated decorative painters to mix and match old ways with new looks. And they're not stopping at paint!

Decoupage, raised gesso surfaces, and the use of metallic leaf take on a completely different look in a contemporary context. Add papier-mâché, mosaics, raffia, wire, beads, even a sense of humor and whimsy, and the looks are unlimited.

This fresh approach finds a natural pairing with unfinished furniture. Affordable, sturdy, and stylish, today's unfinished furniture is a logical choice for a creative painting project.

## How To Use This Book

Nineteen talented designers have created the pieces featured in this book. They've provided step-by-step instructions for successfully completing each project. Full-color photos of each piece, plus close-up shots of design details, will act as your visual guides. If a project features design motifs, you'll find patterns for making templates in the back of the book. All you need to do is copy the motifs for your project, enlarging them to the desired size, and transfer them onto your furniture. (You'll find instructions for transferring on pages 14-15.)

The pieces of unfinished furniture featured in this book are standard styles available in stores throughout the country. If you can't find the exact piece in a store near you, you should be able to find one that closely resembles it. Look for pieces with straight simple lines that will show off the colors and designs. Before you begin, read over the chapters containing basic

information, such as selecting unfinished furniture and the introduction to materials and painting techniques.

Then look over all the projects, pick one you like, read through the directions and start painting.

If you're intimidated by color, don't let this inhibit you from trying a project. For inspiration, clip photographs from current magazines, even if the photos are of a painted wall, landscape, fabric, pottery, floral design, or food. The more you relax and have fun with color, the more willing you'll be to bring it into your life.

## Experiment and Be Adventurous!

If you see a design or technique that you like on a bookcase but need a chair, adapt it—it's easier than you think. Begin by visualizing how a motif would look wrapped around a chair leg, repeated over a tabletop, or stretched along the back slats of a chair. If the design you like has a pattern, copy it, cut it out, then lay it on your furniture or move it around to get an idea of how it will look. You may want to sketch out your ideas first.

Most of all, think of this book as part workbook, part inspiration. Once you complete a piece or two, you should have the confidence to strike out on your own. The object is to have some fun, save money, and fill your living space with furniture that reflects your individual outlook. What a bargain!

# Selecting Unfinished Furniture

## Value with Style

Unfinished furniture is a great value. By finishing a piece yourself, you can save a substantial amount of money compared to the price of a similar piece of pre-finished furniture.

When you walk into an unfinished furniture store you'll find period reproductions, such as Chippendale and Queen Anne, side-by-side with country primitives, Mission, and Shaker-inspired designs. You'll also find a wide selection of contemporary pieces with clean, simple lines that blend easily into today's eclectic interiors.

## New Options for New Looks

For many years, the traditional way of treating unfinished furniture focused on the skills necessary to make a less expensive wood look like a more expensive one.

Within the past 30 years, an interest in lighter, more natural wood finishes has brought about a change in the way people view unfinished furniture. Products that highlighted a wood's grain became popular. Pine, and the other less expensive woods, once thought inferior for fine furniture, became valued for their own versatile and contemporary looks.

Today, the renewed interest in painted furniture and decorative painting techniques, combined with easy-to-use materials, has opened a new era for unfinished furniture. Now, do-it-yourself enthusiasts now have an array of exciting and colorful options available to them.

## About Woods

The furniture in this book is made from solid wood. While you can find unfinished furniture that uses particle board, plywood, and veneers, solid-wood construction gives you a piece that is stronger, longer lasting, and a better investment. You can repaint or refinish solid wood furniture many times over without harming the structure of the piece or the integrity of the wood.

The most common woods used in unfinished furniture are:

**Alder**—a hardwood from the Pacific Northwest of the United States that follows oak and pine as the third most commonly used wood for unfinished furniture.
**Ash**—a hardwood similar in grain pattern to oak.
**Aspen**—a light-colored hardwood with an even grain that is softer than oak.
**Beech**—a tight-grained hardwood that bends well and is used in chairs and stools.
**Oak**—a hardwood with an open grain.
**Parawood**—a wood from the Far East that is as hard as maple with a grain resembling mahogany.
**Pine**—a softwood that comes in many varieties.

Softwoods, as their name implies, are less dense than hardwoods, making them slightly more subject to

dents, nicks, and scratches. If you need a piece to withstand heavy daily use, choose a hardwood; otherwise, for normal daily use, or as an occasional or accessory piece, a softwood will serve you well.

## About Construction

As you look for unfinished furniture, you may notice construction materials and techniques that are different from those used in some prefinished furniture. Though you may not see dovetailing and doweled joints, the durability of unfinished furniture benefits from modern woodworking technology. Pneumatically driven staples coated in resin, precision-fitted metal braces and drawer glides, and strong, high-performance glues are designed to deliver value without sacrificing durability.

Depending on where you purchase your unfinished furniture, it may come either assembled or unassembled. Many stores will charge a small fee for assembling the more complicated pieces. However, you can easily assemble most pieces yourself using a few simple tools. Complete illustrated instructions, along with all the hardware you'll need, are included. Within a few minutes, you'll be ready to paint.

# Tools and Materials

The following will provide you with general information about basic tools and materials. If you've done basic household painting, you may already have many of the supplies you need. If you have to buy anything, you'll find all items are readily available at paint, hardware, and art- or craft-supply stores.

## Brushes

You don't need to invest in specialized decorative painting brushes to create these projects. You'll find that a 2" (5 cm) or 3" (7.5 cm) flat paintbrush, the kind used for household painting, are the most versatile sizes to own. While a straight-edge brush works well on flat surfaces, an angled brush will help you when you want to paint clean straight edges and nice sharp corners. If you're buying, look for brushes with pliable bristles made from a good synthetic or a blend of synthetic bristles and natural animal hair—they're moderately priced and will give you years of wear.

You'll also need a variety of artist's brushes for finer detail work such as outlining, highlighting, and blending. When looking for artist's brushes, you'll find a wide range of prices. Again, a good moderately priced brush should serve you well. Be wary of inexpensive "bargain" brushes—they have a tendency to shed bristles, making them frustrating to work with and can negatively affect the final results of your project.

Remember, brushes are your most important tool. Clean them immediately after each use—this will help them last longer, making them an even better value. Disposable foam brushes in a range of sizes are always handy. You can use them for many different tasks when working with water-based formulas such as applying primer coats, glue, sizing for metallic leaf, or finish coats.

## Carbon or Graphite Transfer Paper

Use this for transferring designs to the surface of your furniture. Carbon paper is black, graphite paper can be black or white.

## Drop Cloths and Old Newspapers

Whether you're working in a well-equipped studio or in a corner of your apartment, you'll need to protect the floor. Use an old sheet, purchase inexpensive drop cloths, or spread out old newspapers before beginning your work.

## Gesso

Gesso is made from chalk powder that is mixed into a liquid medium to create a thick, white, opaque solution. Acrylic gesso is easy to use and cleans up with water. Gesso seals porous surfaces. It can hide any trace of a wood's grain when applied in successive layers, creating a flat, smooth surface desirable in some painting techniques.

## Glaze Medium

A glaze, or wash, is a thin, semi-transparent layer of color. You can thin latex or acrylic paint with water to create a wash, and oil paint with turpentine to create a glaze. However, use of a glaze medium is often recommended.

Glaze medium comes in either water- or oil-based formulas. It extends the color to create the desired semi-transparent effect. It may look milky when you first open it, but dries clear and will not affect the color you mix into it for tinting. You can color glaze medium by using artist's colors, household paint, or dry pigments. Glaze medium is formulated to dry more slowly than paint, providing a longer working time for techniques that call for manipulation of the top coats, such as rag rolling, marbling, stippling, and dry-brushing.

## Metallic Leaf

When thin sheets of beaten metal called "leaf" are applied to a surface, they make an object look as if it is made of gold or silver. While leaf can be made from precious metals, it is also made from other less expensive metals that replicate the look of gold and silver. This less expensive leaf is known as "composition leaf." Leaf is applied to the surface by a glue medium known as "size." The size is applied to the surface, then allowed to dry slightly until it is "tacky" to the touch. The leaf is then laid on the tacky size which adheres it to the surface.

## Paint

Paint is either water-based (acrylic or latex) or oil-based. Water-based paint is almost odorless, cleans up with soap and water, and dries quickly. You can get water-based paint in a range of finishes from matte (a flat no-sheen finish) to high-gloss (which looks like a shiny enamel). Oil-based paint has a stronger "paint" smell, cleans up with mineral spirits or turpentine, and takes longer to dry. Both paints will provide satisfactory results and a durable finish. Water-based paint's ease of use and quick drying time, however, make it the popular choice for most projects.

Artist's acrylics, purchased in tubes or jars, offer other color options. Use them for painting smaller areas, detailing a motif, outlining, and highlighting. Since artist's colors are more concentrated than household paint you may need to thin them with water before use. Artist's colors also work well for tinting glazes.

## Primers

A primer fills and seals the bare wood, providing a better surface for accepting the paint. You can apply a separate sealer before applying the primer, but a good all-purpose primer-sealer formulated for use with water- or oil-based paints is easy to use and easy to clean with soap, water, and household ammonia.

Latex and acrylic paint can act as their own primer. To do this, simply dilute some of the latex or acrylic paint in water, apply, and let dry. Apply all following coats undiluted. The base (first) coat of latex or acrylic paint, when applied directly to the bare wood, can also serve as the primer. However, the little extra time you take to apply a separate primer coat will produce more satisfactory results.

## Rags

Lint-free rags are indispensable when it comes to wiping up drips and spills, and for cleaning brushes. You may also use them barely damp to clean the surface of the wood after sanding and before painting. Old T-shirts make ideal clean-up rags but aren't always lint-free.

## Sandpaper

Sandpaper is referred to by its grade, such as coarse, medium, fine, and extra fine. It may also be referred to by numbers that indicate the amount of grit used per square inch on the sanding surface: #150 to #200 are considered medium grade, while #400 and #600 are fine to extra fine grade.

Sandpaper is further categorized as dry or wet/dry. Dry sandpaper, with a grit made most often of garnet, is suitable for use on bare wood or on painted or varnished surfaces. Wet/dry sandpaper, with a grit of silicon carbide, can be used dry on bare wood or wet with water on paint and varnish. It's used when a fine and flawless look is desired.

## Stains

Stain, as it names implies, soaks into the wood to impart color. Most often labeled with names that characteristically define a wood's color, such as pecan, cherry, walnut, and mahogany, stain also comes in a range of colors, including white.

## Stencils

Stencils can be made from stenciling paper, which resembles thick card stock, or sheets of acetate. You can cut stencils with a sharp utility or craft knife.

## Tack Cloth

A tack cloth is a piece of material that has been treated to make it sticky to the touch and is used to clean the wood's surface. Use it to remove any debris, such as small particles of sand or dirt, after sanding or before you begin painting.

## Tape

Masking tape is used to keep paint contained within certain areas when working on a multi-color design. Standard beige masking tape, found everywhere, has the shortest cure time. This means you can leave it on for about eight hours before the adhesive "cures," making it more difficult to remove. Low-tack, (less sticky) masking tape, with an even longer cure time of three to four days, can be readily found at hardware and paint stores. It is bright blue, making it distinguishable from the other masking tapes. Since it's less tacky, it prevents the paint from being pulled up when removing the tape. Plus, the extended cure time allows you to leave it in place longer so the paint can dry thoroughly. It's desirable for use with many of the layered or hard-edge techniques.

## Varnishes and Protective Coats

When you're through painting, you may want to further protect the surface, add sheen, or tone down shiny surfaces by applying additional coats of clear varnish or polyurethane. Both water- and oil-based formulas are available and come in a range of sheens from matte to high-gloss. Clear spray acrylics, which also come in a variety of sheens, are useful as a finish coat. When using them as a protective finish, you'll need to apply more than one coat.

## Wood Filler

If the wood has small dents or nicks, natural flaws, or nail or staple holes, use wood filler to even the surface before applying the primer coat. Follow the manufacturer's instructions for application.

# Basic Techniques—
## Getting Started

**M**ost projects will be created in three basic stages: preparation, priming, and painting. The general instructions for these stages are given here. For specific information, follow the individual instructions for your chosen project.

## Preparation

The amount of preparation necessary depends on the condition of the wood, the paint or stain you'll be using, and the desired final effect you're trying to achieve. For instance, if you want your piece to have a smooth, flawless finish, you'll spend more time prepping the wood than for a piece that will have an antiqued or distressed look.

Since each technique and piece of wood is different, you'll need to make your own determination about the amount of preparation that's necessary. Always begin by assessing the wood's condition. Look for any surface imperfections, such as naturally occurring flaws or knots; or for any nicks and indentations made in construction, such as holes from screws, nails, or staples; or for any dents or chips made during handling.

If needed, fill the holes and indentations with a suitable wood filler. Follow the manufacturer's directions for application, allowing ample drying time. Once the filler is dry, use a fine-grit sandpaper to remove any excess. Continue sanding the filled patches until they are smooth and even with the surrounding wood.

Whether you use wood filler or not, you will always need to sand the wood. This is very important, since sanding eliminates any minor flaws and makes the surface uniformly smooth. While many manufacturers pre-sand the furniture, it's advisable to do a light sanding of your own.

Begin by looking for any rough patches and edges, or raised areas in the grain. Use a medium-grit sandpaper on the roughest areas to even them into the surrounding surface. Next, using a fine-grit sandpaper, lightly sand the entire surface. Always sand with the grain of the wood, not across it. Use a tack cloth or a barely damp rag to remove any sanding debris.

## Priming

Primer fills and seals the wood. However, don't be tempted to skip the preparation stage in expectation of getting the same results with primer alone that you would get by proper filling and sanding.

While the first coat of acrylic or latex paint can serve as a primer, it's best to use a preparation especially formulated for this purpose. If you're using oil-based paint, use an oil-based sealer—this prevents the first coat of paint from soaking into the raw wood. For most of the projects using latex or acrylic paint, you'll get the best results using all-purpose primer-sealers that clean up with water and household ammonia.

After sanding the raw wood and removing any debris, apply the primer by painting across the grain of the wood rather than with the grain. If you're working with pine that has

knots, and you don't want the knots to show as part of the final effect, take special care to prime them well before painting. Tannin in the wood, which is concentrated in the knots, will eventually bleed through the paint. It's always best to spot seal the knots and any dark areas in the graining with a separate sealer that contains shellac or a spray stain blocker before applying your overall coat of primer.

After the primer coat is dry, lightly sand the surface and remove any debris. If you are applying more than one coat of primer, sand in between each coat.

You can also use gesso as a primer. Because it dries hard, the application of many layers of gesso creates a flat, smooth, and flawless surface necessary for some painting techniques. Even though it's much thicker than standard primer, you can apply it with a brush. Allow the gesso to dry, then sand with a fine-grit sandpaper before applying the paint or the next layer of gesso.

## Painting

After priming, most projects begin with a base coat, the first coat of paint that lays a background color for other techniques. You can save time on a project by tinting the primer the same color as your base coat. You'll have to judge whether this will give you satisfactory results for the desired outcome of the project. If not, apply a base coat of the specified paint as instructed.

If you've chosen a project with design motifs, you'll need to transfer the designs to the wood. The designers have provided patterns on pages 136-142 for making the templates you'll need. First, find the appropriate pattern and copy it using a copy machine, enlarging as necessary to fit your piece of furniture. Lay a piece of carbon or graphite transfer paper, carbon or graphite side down, on the area of the furniture that will be receiving the design. Place the template over the transfer, positioning the template where you want it. Then, using a ballpoint pen, lightly trace over the lines of the design. Do not press too hard—you don't want to make indentations in the wood. Carefully lift the transfer

do not drag it as you would if you were painting. Carefully remove the stencil so the paint won't smear.

Sponge printing is another method designers may use for repeating a motif to create a design. If your project uses this technique, find the pattern you need, transfer it to the sponge, then cut the sponge into that shape. To paint, dip the sponge in the paint and apply to the surface as directed, repeating as necessary to complete the design.

The last part of the painting stage may involve application of a clear finish coat such as sealer or varnish. Other projects may call for further surface treatment involving gluing objects onto the painted wood, decoupage, or distressing the painted surface by sanding for an antiqued or weathered look.

paper off the furniture; avoid sliding it off or it may smudge.

There is an alternate method of transferring the design that involves a few more steps and is handy if you don't have transfer paper readily available. First, copy the design, enlarging if necessary. Using tracing paper, trace the design. Turn the tracing paper over, and, using a #2 or softer pencil, trace the lines of the design once again. Turn the paper over and lay it on the wood in the desired position. Using the pencil, retrace the lines. Carefully lift the tracing paper from the surface to avoid making any smudges on the trans-ferred design.

Some projects use stencils for creating their design motifs. The designers for these projects have provided patterns that will enable you to cut your own. To make a stencil, purchase uncut sheets of stenciling material or use a heavyweight paper that's equivalent to a good card stock. Transfer the pattern to the stenciling material or paper, then, using a craft knife, cut out the design. To paint a stencil, lay the stencil on the desired area of the wood. Use a stencil brush (a short, round, flat-end brush) for applying the paint. Fill the brush with paint— you want to use just enough to avoid any drips. Dab the brush over the stencil;

# Tables

# Children's Checkerboard-Top Table

**K**ids won't have to look far for something to do when their table is also a game board. Bright colors and whimsical motifs make this an inviting piece of furniture in a family room, play space, or kitchen.

*Designer: Esther P. Doyle*

*actual size: 24"w x 24"d x 22"h (61 x 61 x 56 cm)*

## Materials

Square-top table

Primer

Latex semigloss enamel in off-white
and periwinkle blue

Artist's acrylics in cadmium yellow medium,
naphthol crimson, lime-green, ultra blue,

Water-based low-lustre polyurethane.

## Tools

Extra-fine sandpaper

Tack cloth or damp rag

2½" (6.5 cm) angled paintbrush

1" (2.5 cm) flat artist's brush

1" (2.5 cm) trim roller

#8 round acrylic artist's brush

Two small household sponges

Scissors or craft knife

Measuring tape or long ruler

Pencil

**1**

Using the extra-fine sandpaper, sand the table until it's smooth and no rough edges remain.

**2**

Wipe off any dust and debris with a tack cloth or damp rag. Allow to dry if necessary.

**3**

Apply a coat of primer to the table and allow to dry.

**4**

For the base coat, apply two to three coats of off-white latex paint to the tabletop and sides, and periwinkle

blue to the legs. You can quick-dry each coat with a hair dryer, otherwise allow four hours drying time for each coat before applying the next one.

**5**

Using the 1" (2.5 cm) brush, apply two coats of the yellow to opposite sides of the tabletop. To the other two sides, apply the crimson. Multiple coats (at least two) will give you crisp, clean colors. Allow the paint to dry thoroughly between coats.

**6**

Using the 1" (2.5 cm) roller, roll lime-green onto the tabletop edges. Apply two coats, allowing each coat to dry thoroughly before applying the next one.

**7**

With the #8 round artist's brush and off-white paint, make "waves" on two opposite table legs. Rinse the brush.

**8**

Using a scissors or craft knife, cut one of the sponges into a small star shape. Dip the star into a small amount of off-white paint and print onto the other two table legs.

**9**

With the #8 brush and the ultra blue paint, make "slash" marks over red table sides, starting at the bottom edge. Rinse the brush. With the same brush and the crimson paint, make a wave design over the yellow table sides.

**10**

To make dots, dip the tip of the #8 brush handle into an approximately ⅛" (.3 cm) deep puddle of yellow paint. Apply to the green table edges, dipping the tip into the paint to reload when necessary.

**11**

Using the tape measure or ruler and pencil, measure from opposite corners of the tabletop to find the center point and mark it—this is the middle of the table. Measure from the table edge to the center mark. Using this measure, move in 4" (10 cm) from the edges on each side of the table and make a light mark. Draw faint pencil lines connecting these marks through the center point. This will give you your center lines.

**12**

Using a scissors or craft knife, cut the household sponge into a 2" (5 cm) square. Dip it into a shallow puddle of periwinkle blue paint. With one of its ends aligned with one of the pencil lines and its corner at the center mark, lightly press the sponge to the tabletop.

**13**

Position the next sponged square on the opposite side of the line, aligning it with the center line and with its edge just touching the last sponged design. Continue in this zigzag manner until there are four spaces to the left and four spaces to the right of center, for a total of eight spaces across the table (four white and four blue) on each row. Continue in this manner on both sides of the table until there is a total of eight rows of pattern going in each direction. This is a regulation checkerboard or chess board. Allow the paint to dry.

**14**

Apply two coats of polyurethane, allowing the first coat to dry thoroughly before applying the next one.

# Fantastic Faux Leather

**T**his handsome design utilizes an easy faux-painting technique to give the center of the table and the seat of the chair a classic leather look. Add metallic bronze highlights against the black to create a striking contrast, and you have pieces that are dramatically elegant in any setting.

*Designer: Lyna Farkas*

## Materials

Pine table

Pine chair

Acrylic paint in black, bright red, burnt sienna, and metallic bronze

Water-based glaze

Can of clear spray shellac

*actual size: table, 16"w x 16"d x 25"h
(40.5 x 40.5 x 63.5 cm);*

## Tools

| |
|---|
| Fine sandpaper |
| Low-tack painter's masking tape |
| 2" (5 cm) disposable foam brushes |
| Mixing containers |
| 1" 2.5 cm) disposable foam brushes |
| Large new sponge in a plastic wrapper |
| Household sponge |
| Utility knife |
| Plastic wrap |
| Newsprint or rags |

Top

**1**

Lightly sand the table with the fine-grit sandpaper and remove any debris.

**2**

Seal the table with one coat of clear spray shellac.

**3**

Measure 2" (5 cm) in from the edges of the tabletop. Since you'll be painting the black "frame" first, lay the painter's tape on the inside of this borderline to protect the center area.

**4**

Using a 2" (5 cm) foam brush apply the black acrylic paint to the tabletop "frame," then to the remainder of the table, excluding the center square on the tabletop. Let dry.

**5**

Apply a second coat. Let dry.

**6**

Remove the painter's tape and remask the area, this time laying the tape on the outside of the borderline to protect the black "frame."

**7**

Using a 2" (5 cm) foam brush, apply the bright red paint to the center square. Let dry.

**8**

Mix together a dab of the black paint and a dab of burnt sienna. Add this to the water-based glaze in the proportion of one part paint to two parts glaze.

**9**

With one of the disposable brushes, stroke a few random brush marks of this mixture over the red square.

**10**

Keeping the large sponge in its plastic wrapper, use it to move the paint and glaze mixture around by patting it in different directions until it gives a consistent leather appearance. Carefully remove the tape and let dry.

## 11

With the utility knife, cut a 1¾" (4.5 cm) square and a 1¾ x 3¼" (4.5 x 8.5 cm) rectangle from the household sponge.

## 12

Brush the bronze paint on one side of each sponge with a 1" (2.5 cm) foam brush, then press this side to the black border in a pattern of your choosing. The pattern used for this project was one square at each corner with three rectangles on each side. Have fun with this—don't worry about being exact.

## 13

Continue printing on the sides of the table. The pattern used for this project was square, rectangle, square. Allow the paint to dry.

## 14

Apply a coat of clear spray shellac to the table.

## CHAIR

## 1

Follow Steps 1-10 for the table instructions, adapting the measurements to the shape of the seat.

## 2

Using a utility knife, cut a 1¾ x 3¼" (4.5 x 8.5 cm) rectangle out of the household sponge.

## 3

Brush the bronze acrylic paint on one side of sponge with the 1" (2.5 cm) foam brush. Press this painted side to the black "frame" around the seat, spacing evenly as you continue around. Again, don't be too concerned with being exact— have fun with this.

## 4

Press the painted sponge three times across the seat back.

## 5

Bunch up a small amount of plastic wrap and dab it in the red paint, patting any excess on newsprint or rags. Pat the paint-coated plastic wrap around the inner rungs beneath the seat, letting patches of black show through. Allow the paint to dry.

## 6

Apply a coat of clear spray shellac to the chair.

*actual size: chair, 15½"w x 18½"d x 34"h
(39.5 x 47 x 86.5 cm)*

# Fiddleback Grain with Scratch Finish

*actual size: 30"w x 14"d x 33"h (76 x 35.5 x 84 cm)*

C ombine a simple glaze technique that duplicates the grain pattern of maple used for making fiddlebacks with a scratched "metallic" finish to create this handsome piece. Though the console table is designed to be placed against a wall, it will be a standout in any location.

*Designer: Kevin Fulford*

## Materials

| |
|---|
| Table |
| Wood filler |
| All-purpose primer |
| Latex paint, satin-finish in white and creamy yellow |
| Oil glaze |
| Linseed oil |
| Odorless paint thinner |
| Mixing containers |
| Artist's oil colors in raw sienna, burnt umber, blue, red, and black |
| Clear acrylic varnish |
| Steel wool, medium grade |

## Tools

| |
|---|
| Fine-grit sandpaper |
| Rags |
| Tack cloth |
| 2" or 3" (5 or 7.5 cm) paintbrushes |
| 3" (7.5 cm) bristle brush |
| Pencil |
| Paper |
| Transfer paper |
| Low-tack painter's tape |
| Scissors |

**1**

Fill any imperfections in the wood with wood filler, allow to dry, then sand the patches smooth with fine-grit sandpaper. Sand the entire piece lightly with fine-grit sandpaper, removing any debris with a tack cloth or damp rag.

**2**

Seal any knots until they no longer bleed through the primer- sealer or shellac. Apply a coat of all-purpose primer and allow to dry.

**3**

Apply a base coat of the satin-finish white latex paint and allow to dry.

**4**

To make the curving lines, first sketch the design on paper, then use transfer paper to transfer the lines to the table. (See pages 14-15 for transferring instructions.) Make sure the curving lines extend to the table's sides and back.

**5**

Since you'll be painting the bottom of the table first, use the painter's tape to mask the top of the design. To follow the curvature of the lines, tear the tape in small pieces before applying to the lines. You may need to use scissors to make small clips in the tape to get it to fit the curves.

## 6

Paint the bottom part with satin-finish creamy yellow latex and allow to dry.

## 7

Thin the oil glaze with a small amount of linseed oil. Take one part of this thinned glaze and mix it with one part odorless paint thinner. Divide this glaze mixture into two separate portions and set one aside. To one portion add the artist's oil colors in raw sienna and burnt umber. This will give you the color for the graining—you don't want to make it too dark.

## 8

For the fiddleback technique, work one section at a time—don't attempt to apply the glaze all at once. *Note:* As with any unfamiliar technique, it's best to practice on paper or a scrap of wood first before painting the piece. Apply the glaze over one section of the yellow paint. Using the 3" (7.5 cm) bristle brush, simply "rock" the brush side to side while lightly dragging it through the glaze. Since you want to keep the brush fairly dry, wipe it on a rag to remove any excess glaze as you work. Choose one direction to move in for a consistent pattern. Repeat the technique on all sections and allow the glaze to dry completely.

## 9

Varnish the grained pattern with an acrylic clear coat, allow to dry, then remove the tape.

## 10

Once you remove the tape, there may be an edge of paint on the tape line. Use the fine-grit sandpaper to remove any paint residue from this line.

## 11

For the metallic technique on the top, mix the other portion of thinned glaze made in Step 7 with artist's oil color in blue and red to get a light blue-purple color. To this, add just a bit of black to darken slightly.

## 12

Working a section at a time (top, sides, front, and back), use a regular paintbrush to apply the purple glaze to the white top half of the table. At the curving line, use the brush to carefully cut in next to the existing fiddleback finish.

## 13

Using a clean rag, dab at the wet glaze for a mottled effect that will give you some contrasting light and dark areas. Then, use the bristle brush to lightly blend these areas together.

## 14

Using medium-grade steel wool, lightly swipe it through the glaze in all directions. When too much glaze collects on the steel wool, discard that piece, using a clean piece to continue working. When you finish "scratching," clean any excess glaze off the curvy line on the fiddleback finish. Allow the glaze to dry completely.

## 15

When the glaze is dry, varnish the entire table with clear acrylic varnish.

# Frog Table

**T**he small frog hiding in the leaves adds a surprising highlight to the lush background colors and the strong lines of this design. For textural interest, you'll learn a simple decorative painting technique for adding depth to the base color.

*Designer: Bess Baird*

## Materials

Table

Gloss gel medium

Semi-gloss latex paint in red-orange

Acrylic artist's colors in violet, blue-green, and yellow

White latex primer

White latex paint

Water-based varnish

## Tools

Four small glass jars with lids

2" (5 cm) paintbrushes

#320 sandpaper

Tack cloth

Damp rags

Carbon transfer paper

Pencil

Low-tack painter's masking tape

Medium-sized plastic bags—shopping bags from the grocery store work best

Rubber comb for decorative painting, found in paint and craft stores

¼" (.5 cm) flat, short-haired artist's brush

*The pattern for this design is on page 142.*

**1**

Mix four glazes using the red-orange latex paint and the acrylic artist's colors in violet, blue-green, and yellow. To do this, place some gloss gel medium into each small jar. Add the colors, one to each jar, mix, cover, and set aside.

**2**

Using the white primer, paint the table and let dry.

**3**

Since water-based primer tends to raise the grain of the wood, lightly sand the surface of the primed table. Remove any debris using a tack cloth or damp rag.

**4**

Paint the table with white paint and let dry.

**5**

Using the transfer paper and the pattern, transfer the design to the tabletop. (See page 000 for transferring instructions.) If you have a steady hand and good eye, use a pencil to copy the design by drawing it directly on the table top.

**6**

Using the masking tape, mask the copied design in order to paint the background. Seal the edges of the tape well.

**7**

Paint the top, the legs, and shelf with the red-orange latex paint. Remove the tape and use a damp rag to carefully wipe away any paint that has seeped onto the copied design. Let dry.

**8**

Using the masking tape, retape the copied design, sealing the edges well. Beginning with the top of the table, paint over all the red-orange surfaces with the violet glaze, including the legs and shelf. Crumple a plastic bag and quickly pat it all over the glazed areas. Remove the tape from the top and use a damp rag to carefully wipe away any paint that has seeped onto the copied design. Let dry.

**9**

Paint the panels below the tabletop with violet glaze and let dry.

**10**

Paint the panels again with violet glaze. Following the technique in Step 8, quickly pat the glazed surface with a crumpled plastic bag. Let dry.

**11**

On the tabletop, use the masking tape to tape the red-orange background to expose two or three leaves of the design that do not touch each other.

**12**

Paint the leaves with violet glaze. With the glaze wet, take the rubber comb and drag it through each leaf. Remove the tape carefully from the background. Use a damp rag to wipe away any glaze that has seeped onto the background. Let dry. Continue this process until all the leaves been painted. Let dry.

**13**

Paint over the violet-striped leaves with the blue-green glaze. Let dry.

**14**

Paint the underside of the leaves with violet glaze. Note: The leaves have two parts, a top side and an underside. Each are painted differently.

**15**

With the ¼" (.5 cm) brush, paint the circles on the base of the plant using the four glazes. To make a circle, place a small amount of glaze on the brush, lay the brush on its side, and quickly make a circle. Fill in the area with circles made of the different colors.

**16**

Using all four glaze colors, hand paint the frog using the photograph as a visual guide.

**17**

When all paint is completely dry, apply the water-based varnish as a finish coat.

**TIPS:**

• Even though the masking tape is low-tack, always lift it carefully when removing it from a painted surface.

• To mask complicated lines and strong curves, use a translucent painter's tape to give you an exact fit. Lay the tape on top of a drawn line, then use a pencil to trace the line on the tape. Use a craft knife to cut along the traced line, removing the tape from the area to be painted.

• Plan ahead as you work to avoid working on an area that is next to a wet area.

# Children's Table and Chairs

**D**esigner Molly Tilden Rousey has gotten to the heart of a child's imagination with this table and chair design. The table's top surface is decorated with a fantasy road for play with small toy cars and figures. Then, after a hard morning of make believe, crawl under the table and look up. There, waiting for you, is a friendly sky—a perfect place for a sweet, dreamy nap.

*Designer: Molly Tilden Rousey*

*actual size: table, 24"w x 18"d x 18¾"h (61 x 45.5 x 48 cm); chairs, 14½"w x 12"d x 24½"h (37 x 30.5 x 62 cm)*

## Materials

Child's table and two chairs

Latex satin-finish paint, 1 quart (1 L) each, in royal blue, red, black, light blue, orange, white, purple, yellow, aqua, green, and brown

Carbon transfer paper

1 quart (1 L) of high-gloss polyurethane

## Tools

2" (5 cm) paintbrush

1" (2.5 cm) paintbrush

Artist's fine-tip, detail brush

1" (2.5 cm) masking tape

*Patterns for this design are on pages 136-137.*

**1**

Paint the underside of the table with two coats of light blue paint. Note: For this step, and for all steps calling for two coats of paint, always allow the first coat to dry thoroughly before applying the second one.

**2**

Paint two of the table legs orange, and the other two red. Apply two coats of each color.

**3**

Paint the seat of one chair (top and underside) green. Paint the seat of the other chair royal blue. Apply two coats of each color.

**4**

Paint the legs of the green-seat chair royal blue. Paint the legs of the blue-seat chair green. Apply two coats of each color.

**5**

Using orange and red paint, paint the rungs and backs of the chairs, alternating the two colors. Apply two coats of each color.

**6**

On the tabletop, using the photograph as a visual guide for placement, sketch out the areas for the pond, road, bridges, and grass. Paint the pond light blue, the road yellow, the grass green, and the bridges brown. Apply two coats of each color.

**7**

Paint the edges of the table white. Apply two coats.

**8**

When the paint is dry, use carbon paper to transfer the patterns for the cars, boat, boat sail, fish, flowers, star,

sun, and clouds to the table and chairs. Use the photograph as a visual guide for placement.

**9**

Paint inside the outlines for each shape with one coat of white paint. This will serve as a base coat for painting the individual designs, blocking out the colors underneath.

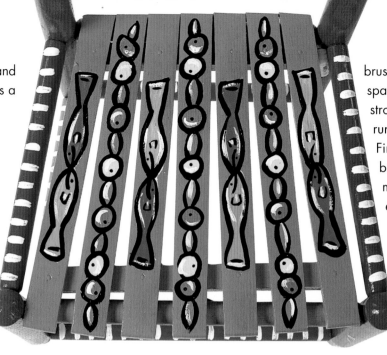

**10**

When the white paint is dry, go back and paint each object. Using the photograph as a visual guide, paint the cars red and royal blue; the fish purple, light blue, orange, and red; the star yellow; the sun yellow and orange; the clouds white; the flowers yellow, light blue, and purple with green leaves; the boat orange; and the sail of the boat white.

**11**

When all the paint is thoroughly dry, use the fine-tip brush to paint black outlines around the objects and the details for each object as shown in their patterns.

**12**

Using the 1" (2.5 cm) masking tape, space small pieces of tape 1" (2.5 cm) apart on the white edges of the table. Seal the edges of the tape well so the paint won't bleed underneath.

**13**

Using black paint, paint between the pieces of tape, allowing the paint to dry before removing the tape.

**14**

Use the fine-tip brush and white paint to highlight and outline each patterned object. Use light and suggestive strokes—do not use any solid lines. Using the same

brush and paint, evenly space short brush strokes across the rungs of the chairs. Finally, with the same brush and paint, make swirls on each end of the stars on the table legs.

**15**

Allow the paint to dry for 24 hours before applying two to three coats of polyurethane for the finish. Allow each coat of polyurethane to dry thoroughly before applying the next one.

# Triangular Night Stand

**T**he triangular shape of this corner table caught the designer's eye and imagination. By turning the table around for use backwards, she created a great night stand. The addition of the balls and the glass top made the table a perfect complement to the height of her bed.

*Designer: Maureen Donahue*

*actual size: 26"w x 13"d x 25"h (66 x 33 x 63.5 cm)*

## Materials

Corner table

Wood filler

Off-white latex paint

Gold paint

Three 2" (5 cm) dia. wooden balls

Three 1 x ¼"(2.5 x .5 cm) wooden dowel pins

Wood glue

Variety of paint colors

¼" (.5 cm) glass cut to a size 1" (2.5 cm)
larger than tabletop—when cut, ask that
the ends be polished

## Tools

Putty knife

Sandpaper in fine and extra-fine grit

Drill with ¼" (.5 cm) drill bit

Vise

2" (5 cm) paintbrush

¾" (2 cm) artist's brush

Stencil, household sponge, or foam

Craft knife or scissors

Cosmetic sponge

### 1

Using the putty knife, fill any imperfections in the wood with wood filler, allow to dry, then sand the patches smooth. Sand the entire table with fine-grit sandpaper, removing any debris.

### 2

Paint the base coat using the 2" (5 cm) brush and the off-white latex paint. When the paint is dry, sand the table using the extra-fine grit sandpaper and remove any debris. Apply a second coat of paint.

### 3

Following the photograph as a visual guide, use a craft knife to cut a stencil of the swirl motif. You can also use scissors to cut a stamp of the motif from a household sponge or piece of foam. If you're using a stencil, use the cosmetic sponge to apply the gold paint. Lay the stencil on the legs in a random pattern— be sure to wrap some of the designs around the edges. If you're using a sponge or foam stamp, dip them in the gold paint and sponge print the design on the legs in the same patterning as described for stenciling.

### 4

Using the drill and bit, drill a ¼" (.5 cm) hole in each ball. For easier handling, secure the balls in a vise before drilling. Make the hole approximately ½" (1.5 cm) deep. Coat one end of each wooden dowel pin with wood glue and insert them into the holes in each ball. Allow the glue to dry. Using the ¾" (2 cm) artist's brush, paint each ball a different color, allowing the paint to dry thoroughly.

### 5

Using the same drill bit, drill a hole into each corner of the table, approximately ½" (1.5 cm) deep. As you did for the balls, coat the ends of the dowels with wood glue and insert into the holes in the table.

### 6

Set the glass on top of the balls.

# Tissue Paper Hall Table

**T**his table can be customized to give you the look you want. For an overall parchment effect, stop once you've applied the paper patterns. For extra highlights, add the colored tissue. For more interest, use rubber-stamp letters to have the final word.

*Designer: Ellen Zahorec*

## Materials

| |
|---|
| Table |
| Dress patterns |
| Tissue paper in yellow and orange |
| 1 can spray adhesive |
| Water-based polyurethane in either shiny, matte, or semigloss finish |
| Rubber-stamp letters |
| Black acrylic craft paint, or India ink |

## Tools

| |
|---|
| Fine-grit sandpaper |
| Tack cloth |
| Scissors |
| 2" or 3" (5 or 7.5 cm) disposable foam brushes |

**1**

Sand the table, removing any debris with the tack cloth.

**2**

Using a disposable foam brush, coat the table with the polyurethane.

*actual size: 31"w x 11"d x 30"h*
*(78.5 x 28 x 76 cm)*

**3**

Working while the polyurethane is still wet, rip and/or cut the dress patterns, then lay the pieces at random on the table. As you lay them, keep them as smooth as possible, trying to avoid any bubbles or wrinkles in the paper. You may need an extra pair of hands to help you—the paper is so thin it blows in the slightest breeze, making it tricky to handle. Cover the whole table, overlapping the pieces as you work.

**4**

Without letting the polyurethane dry, gently brush more polyurethane on top of the first layer of tissue paper. Apply another layer as you did in Step 3.

**5**

Without letting the polyurethane dry, gently brush more polyurethane on top of the second layer of tissue. Allow the polyurethane to dry. You can stop here and your table will have an overall "parchment" look, or you can continue and add the colored tissue for extra highlights and detail.

**6**

Cut the colored tissue to fit the areas of the table you'll be covering—yellow for the legs and orange for the sides and top.

**7**

Spray the adhesive directly on the table and apply the tissue. Use scissors to trim

any excess tissue. Repeat for all areas of the table to be covered.

**8**

Apply a coat of polyurethane to the entire table and allow to dry. Tissue paper colors will bleed when wet. To avoid coloring adjoining areas, you may want to use separate disposable foam brushes for applying the polyurethane to the different areas of the table.

**9**

You can stop here, or you can further embellish the table by applying words. To do this, dip the rubber-stamp letters in black acrylic paint that has been thinned slightly with water or in India ink. Stamp the words on the table and allow to dry.

**10**

You may want to apply a final coat of polyurethane for extra protection. Since you already sealed the tissue colors in Step 8, you can use one brush for this application.

# Paper Napkin Collage Table

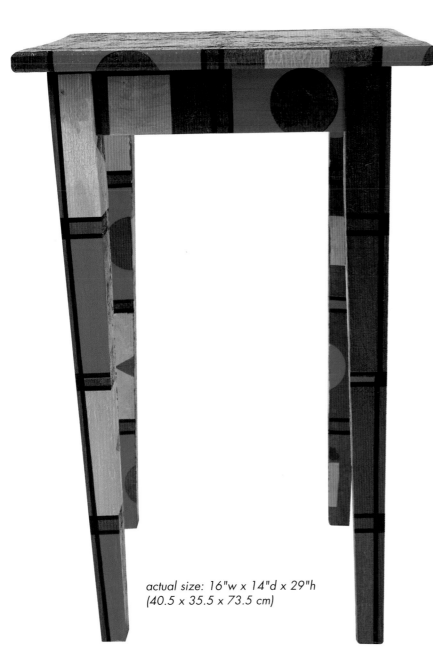

*actual size: 16"w x 14"d x 29"h (40.5 x 35.5 x 73.5 cm)*

**S**elections in paper napkins are almost endless—florals, geometrics, novelties. With this technique, you can create a table to fit just about any style, mood, or occasion based on the design you choose. Adapt this project using fabric for even more versatility.

*Designer: Ellen Zahorec*

## Materials

Small table

Paper napkins

Water-based polyurethane

## Tools

Fine-grit sandpaper

Tack cloth

Scissors

2" or 3" (5 or 7.5 cm) disposable foam brushes.

**1**

Sand the table, removing any debris with the tack cloth.

**2**

The napkins selected for this design were very expensive, but very wonderful. Find napkins that inspire you!

**3**

Since most paper napkins are two or three ply, separate the layers, removing all but the top layer. The paper will be very thin, soft, and easily shredded, so be careful when handling it.

**4**

Depending on the size and design of the napkin you selected, either keep it whole or cut it into sections. You may want to spend some time beforehand deciding how to build your design. Some floral and special-occasion napkins will look good if randomly applied, while using geometrics and blocks of colors on your table may need some planning.

**5**

Coat the table with the polyurethane.

**6**

Working while the polyurethane is still wet, apply the napkins to the table by laying them in place one at a time. Once you lay a napkin, gently brush over the top of it with the polyurethane. Don't worry if you shred an area, you can go back and patch it later when you apply the second layer. Completely cover the table in this manner following your design.

**7**

Allow the polyurethane to dry completely before applying a second layer of napkins following the procedure in Step 6. If desired, allow the polyurethane to dry completely and apply a third layer.

**8**

When you've finished layering the paper to your satisfaction, and have allowed the polyurethane to dry, apply a final coat of polyurethane and allow to dry.

**TIP:** For a slightly different look, prime the table after sanding, then apply a base coat of color. If the napkins rip, tear, or shred when you're applying them, do not correct this, allowing the base color to show through as an added design element.

Top

# Tiled Table

**Y**ou won't have to worry about water stains on this tabletop. With mosaic tiles and a little time, you can transform a wooden table into a handy accessory for use in the kitchen or on a covered porch or deck. Buy the mosaic tiles in sheets on a net backing and cut to size, or apply individual tiles for a custom design.

*Designer: Traci Dee Neil-Taylor*

*actual size: 16"w x 14"d x 29"h*
*(40.5 x 35.5 x 73.5 cm)*

## Materials

Table

All-purpose primer-sealer

Latex semigloss paint in colors of your choice to complement the tile colors

Mosaic tiles in colors of your choice

Adhesive

Grout

## Tools

Newspapers

Fine-grit sandpaper

Tack cloth

2" (5 cm) paintbrush

Putty knife or trowel

Sponge

Lint-free rag

**1**

Lay newspapers on the floor to protect it from any spills or drips.

**2**

Lightly sand the table with the fine-grit sandpaper and remove any debris with the tack cloth.

**3**

Apply a coat of primer-sealer and allow to dry.

**4**

Paint the table the desired color and let dry for 24 hours.

**5**

Apply adhesive to the tabletop. You may need to smooth it using a putty knife or small trowel. Apply additional adhesive to the mosaic tiles, either on the back of the net backing or the back of the individual tiles, and place the tiles on the table in the desired pattern. Allow the glue to dry for 24 hours.

**6**

If you're using dry grout, mix the grout according to the manufacturer's instructions. Apply the grout to the top of the tiles with a damp sponge, making sure the grout gets down into all the cracks between the tiles. Use a damp sponge to wipe away any excess grout. Allow the grout to dry for two hours, then use a clean, damp sponge to wipe away any remaining grout residue.

**7**

Wipe the tiles dry with a lint-free rag.

**TIP:** You can change the look of this project by using larger tiles or colored grout. If you use larger tiles, you may need to use tile cutters, found in hardware stores, to trim the tiles to fit. Another option is to use pieces of broken pottery, beach glass, or shells as the tiles in your design.

# Zigzags, Triangles, Xs and Os

"**I** started making diagonal lines on the sides of the legs and went wild," says designer Ellen Zahorec. "The more I filled in and overlapped the lines and colors, the better it got. This is simple but time consuming—think of it as a meditation process."

*Designer: Ellen Zahorec*

*actual size: 16"w x 16"d x 25"h*
*(40.5 x 40.5 x 63.5 cm)*

Top

## Materials

| |
|---|
| Table |
| All-purpose primer |
| Acrylic craft paint or spray acrylic paint in colors of your choice |
| Enamel markers (oil-based) in colors of your choice |
| Water-based polyurethane |

## Tools

| |
|---|
| Fine-grit sandpaper |
| Tack cloth |
| 2" (5 cm) paintbrush |

**1**

Using the fine-grit sandpaper, sand the table, removing any debris with the tack cloth.

**2**

Apply a coat of primer, and allow to dry.

**3**

Using the acrylic craft paint or spray acrylic paint, paint each leg and the top with a different color. This table was done using acrylic craft paint that was brushed on. Allow the paint to dry.

**4**

Working in a well-ventilated area, use the enamel markers to paint the design. Follow the photograph as a visual guide or create your own design. Begin on the legs by making diagonal lines and go from there. If you want, you can gently pencil in the design to help you as you paint with the markers.

**5**

When the design is complete to your satisfaction, apply two coats of polyurethane, allowing the first coat to dry completely before applying the second one.

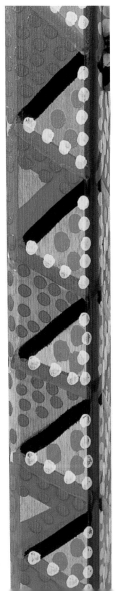

Leg

# Decoupage Table

**D**esigner Ellen Zahorec's inspiration for this table was an architectural plan for a cathedral that she found in an art history book. Then, as she tells it, she "went to the copy shop, and got crazy with the enlarger!"

*Designer: Ellen Zahorec*

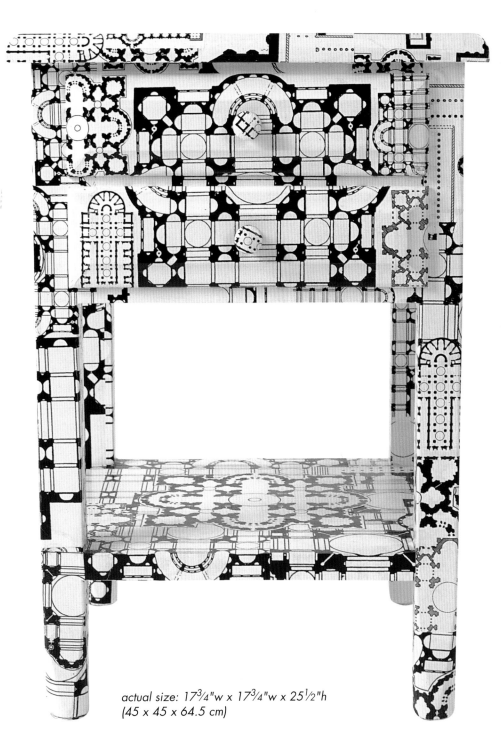

*actual size: 17³/₄"w x 17³/₄"w x 25¹/₂"h*
*(45 x 45 x 64.5 cm)*

## Materials

Table

Historic architectural plans

All-purpose primer-sealer

1 can spray adhesive

Water-based polyurethane in either shiny, matte, or semigloss finish

## Tools

Copy machine

Fine-grit sandpaper

Tack cloth

Scissors

2" or 3" (5 or 7.5 cm) disposable foam brushes

**1**

Find your designs and copy them, enlarging them as necessary to fit your table. Make several copies. If your designs are in color, you can make color copies but they will be more expensive. You can also tint the copies, using markers or colored pencils. However, the stark black and white creates a handsome statement.

**2**

Determine the placement of the designs on the table. All you need is a general idea—random placement is also fine. You may have to play with this, moving the plans around until you get a placement you like, then cut the designs out accordingly.

**3**

Remove the knobs from the drawers. Lightly sand the table, removing any debris with a tack cloth.

**4**

Apply one coat of all-purpose primer-sealer to the table and knobs, and allow to dry.

**5**

Working in a room with adequate ventilation, use the spray adhesive to spray the backs of the papers and apply to the table. *Do not spray the table with adhesive first*—this will prevent any overlapping edges of the paper from adhering to the table. Press each piece of paper to the table, smoothing any wrinkles or bubbles as you work. Don't worry if you make mistakes, you can simply cover them over with another piece of paper.

**6**

Following the same procedure, apply small bits of the designs to the knobs.

**7**

Using a disposable foam brush, apply two to three coats of the polyurethane to the decoupaged table and knobs. Allow each coat to dry thoroughly before applying the next one.

**8**

Replace the knobs.

# Faux Pizza Table

**R**eminiscent of those old-time Italian cafes—complete with its own red and white checkered tablecloth—this pizza table will make you hungry just looking at it. It's fun and easy to create, and will be a favorite for all the pizza lovers in your life.

*Designer: Anne McCloskey*

*actual size: 13½" in diameter x 24"h (34 x 61 cm)*

## Materials

Small round table

Acrylic varnish

Acrylic craft paints in white, light gold, red, red-brown, tan, dark brown, and brown

Paper

## Tools

Fine-grit sandpaper

Tack cloth

2" (5 cm) disposable foam brushes

Small sea sponge

Scissors

Pencil

Two medium artist's brushes—one round, one flat

Household sponge

Paper towels

### 1

Using the fine-grit sandpaper, sand the table to remove any rough spots or edges, then use the tack cloth to remove any debris.

### 2

With a foam brush, coat the top, sides, and legs of the table with varnish. Allow to dry.

### 3

Apply two coats of white paint to the legs, allowing the first coat to dry completely before applying the second one. Allow to dry.

### 4

Apply two coats of light gold paint to the top of the table, including the sides. Allow to dry.

### 5

Wet the small sea sponge until slightly damp, then dip it in the brown paint. Sponge paint the edges of the top and around the sides. Do not apply the paint evenly, it needs to look like it has been "browned" in the oven.

### 6

Cut approximately ten to fifteen 1¾" (4.5 cm) circles out of paper. Lay them on the tabletop, arranging them like pepperoni on a pizza. Lightly trace around them and remove. Use the round artist's brush to apply the light gold, tan, red-brown, and dark brown to each circle. To blend the colors, use a swirling motion as you apply the paint. Make sure each piece of "pepperoni" is different by swirling the colors in different directions and by using more of one color than another.

### 7

The "cheese" is created by building up layers of the tan, brown, and red-brown paint. Make washes of the tan and brown by adding water to each color. You want to thin the paint enough to achieve a

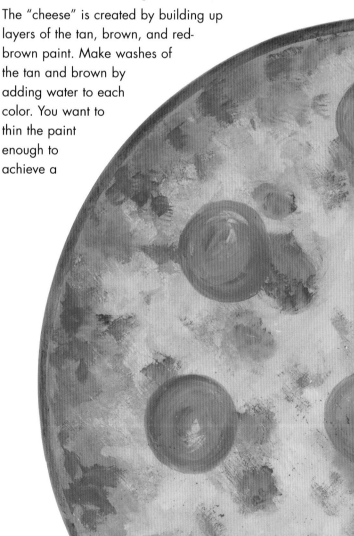

see-through effect. Apply the tan and brown washes around the circles. Allow to dry. Using a dry brush, apply blotchy strokes of red-brown and brown to the areas between the circles. Stand back to see if it looks like a pizza. You may have to rework some places to get the desired effect. Allow to dry. If you're not happy with an area, simply paint over it.

### 8

Cut a household sponge into a 1" (2.5 cm) square and a 1 x ¾" (2.5 x 2 cm) rectangle.

### 9

To paint the legs, dampen the 1" (2.5 cm) sponge square and dip it in the red paint. Blot any excess paint onto a paper towel. Press the square to the top of one side of a table leg. Move the sponge down 1" (2.5 cm), leaving a 1" (2.5 cm) square of white, then print another red square. Continue alternating red and white down the leg's side. When you begin printing on the adjoining side of the leg, make sure you have a white square next to the red one you'll be

printing. Complete all four sides of one leg, then repeat the procedure on the remaining three legs.

### 10

For the table sides, use the 1 x ¾" (2.5 x 2 cm) sponge rectangle to make the red squares. Create the checkerboard effect by alternating red and white to create two horizontal rows on each side. Allow to dry.

### 11

Using a foam brush, apply varnish to the legs, sides, and top of the table, and allow to dry. For added protection, apply a second coat of varnish.

# Painted Floral Table

**T**his sunny and free design brings a fresh look to a small table. Designer Deborah Cavenaugh uses brush strokes that are easy to duplicate, giving the table an artistic, painterly look.

*Designer: Deborah Cavenaugh*

*actual size: 16"w x 16"d x 25"h (40.5 x 40.5 x 63.5 cm)*

## Materials

Pine table

All-purpose white primer-sealer, 1 quart (1 L)

Acrylic artist's colors, 1 small tube each, in golden ocher (sunflower gold), quinachrinone red (rose red), thalo blue (dark sky blue), thalo green (spruce green), and black

Transfer paper—optional

Water-based polyurethane, 1 quart (1 L)

## Tools

Fine-grit sandpaper

Tack cloth

Two 2" (5 cm) disposable foam brushes

Ruler

Pencil

Artist's brushes—#8 round and #2 round lining brush

*Patterns for this design are on page 136.*

### 1

With the fine-grit sandpaper, sand the table, using a tack cloth to remove any debris.

### 2

Spot seal any knots first to prevent them from bleeding through the paint. Using a disposable brush, prime the table with two coats of the all-purpose white primer-sealer. Allow the first coat to dry completely, sand lightly, and remove any debris before applying the second coat.

### 3

To create the border around the tabletop, use a ruler and pencil to measure and draw a line ¾" (2 cm) in

Top

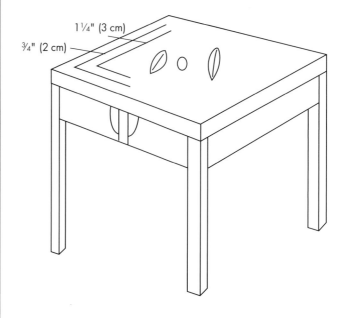

1¼" (3 cm)

¾" (2 cm)

from the edges of the table. Then measure and draw a second line 1¼" (3 cm) in from the edges.

**4**

Copy the leaf and dot patterns for this design and cut them out. Scatter them inside the border, positioning them where you want and trace around their edges. Use as many as you like—you can't have too many or too few.

**5**

Using the #8 brush, paint one side of each leaf thalo blue and the other side thalo green, then paint the border and the dots quinachrinone red.

**6**

Using the pattern or working freehand, transfer or draw five of the leaf variations on the sides of the table.

**7**

Using the #8 brush, paint the longer center of each leaf variation quinachrinone red, paint one side thalo blue, and the other thalo green. Allow to dry.

**8**

Thin the golden ocher slightly with water. Use this color to paint every area of the table that is not already painted, including the areas between the motifs on the tabletop. Allow to dry. Note: When thinning the paint, don't thin it too much since you want the "painterly" brush strokes to show.

**9**

Thin a bit of the quinachrinone red slightly and paint the edges of the top with it. Allow to dry.

**10**

Using the #2 liner brush, outline all the drawn objects (except the border) in black. On the blue sides of the leaves on the tabletop, paint three black slashes.

**11**

Allow all paint to dry overnight.

**12**

Using the fine-grit sandpaper, lightly sand the gold on the legs to allow more white of the primer to show through. Be careful to avoid sanding down to the wood. Remove any debris.

**13**

Using a foam brush, apply two coats of polyurethane, allowing the first coat to dry completely before applying the next one.

# Chef's Cart

Try drawing in paint to create this unique etched look. This technique lends just the right amount of interest to this chef's cart—making it an attractive and practical addition to any busy kitchen.

*Designer: Loveeta Baker*

actual size: 28¼"w x 17"d x 36"h
(72 x 43 x 91.5 cm)

## Materials

| |
|---|
| Chef's cart |
| Oil-based stain in a color of your choice (but not too dark)* |
| Oil-based sealer |
| Oil paint |
| Oil-based polyurethane |
| Paint thinner |

## Tools

| |
|---|
| Sandpaper in fine and medium grit |
| 2" (5 cm) paintbrushes |
| Masking tape |
| Old newspapers |
| Drawing tool—can be a pencil eraser or cotton swabs |
| Rags |

*Although the designer prefers working with oil-based stain, sealer, and paint, you can get comparable results using water-based products. If you do this, make sure that the stain, sealer, and polyurethane you use are compatible with your paint. Read labels and ask for help at the paint store when buying your products.

**Note:** Since the chopping block will come in direct contact with food, it requires special treatment. *Do not stain, seal, paint, or varnish this part of the piece.* Cooking supply shops carry special preparations for conditioning chopping blocks and cutting boards. You can also condition it using mineral oil, *not mineral spirits.* To do this, use a clean rag to apply the mineral oil to the chopping block. Let the oil soak into the wood, wiping away any excess with a clean rag, then allow the block to dry before use. Periodically apply mineral oil to keep the block in good condition.

**1**

Lightly sand all but the chopping block with fine-grit sandpaper. Using a tack cloth, remove any debris. Following the manufacturer's instructions, apply the stain and allow to dry. Again, following the manufacturer's instructions, apply the sealer and allow to dry.

**2**

Using masking tape, and old newspapers if necessary, mask off (cover) all areas on the piece that will not be painted.

**3**

If your piece of furniture is on wheels, as this one is, position it to prevent it from rolling away as you work. Secure it for stability, placing it at an angle or in a position that is comfortable for drawing. You might find it helpful to lay the cart top down, then paint the side facing you first.

**4**

Paint one section using broad even strokes. Do not thin the paint—you want it to be thick enough to be "drawable."

**5**

After applying the paint, use your drawing tool immediately to etch your design into the paint. You may want to practice this technique beforehand on a scrap of wood or heavyweight paper. As you work, use a rag to wipe off any excess paint from the drawing tool—this will help avoid any buildup that can cause smears.

**6**

After you've painted and drawn on all sections, allow the piece to dry completely.

**7**

As an optional surface treatment, use medium- to fine-grit sandpaper on the painted areas to achieve a worn, aged look. If you like the look of the piece just painted and drawn, don't sand it!

**8**

For a protective finish, apply a coat of polyurethane.

**9**

Clean your brushes with paint thinner and rags.

**TIP:** Don't be too concerned about mistakes in your drawing—they often add to the overall look. Learn to live with them. Trying to paint over mistakes, then redrawing, usually causes many more problems than just letting it be in the first place.

# Trompe L'Oeil Teatime Table

Y ou'll find this little table is as much fun to make as it is to use. It's a great conversation piece when entertaining. You might want to consider making it as a wedding, anniversary, or birthday gift for a special person.

*Designer: Anne McCloskey*

*actual size: 13"w x 9¼"d x 22½"h
(33 x 23.5 x 57 cm)*

## Materials

Small rectangular wooden table

Acrylic varnish

Acrylic craft paints in black, light blue, lavender, peri-winkle pink, light pink, yellow-orange, and gray

Two rectangular Battenburg lace place mats

Decoupage medium

Heavyweight paper or cardstock

Teaspoon

Muslin, 18" (45.5 cm)

Two 1" (2.5 cm) dome buttons

Strong adhesive glue

## Tools

Fine-grit sandpaper

Tack cloth

Two 2" (5 cm) disposable foam brushes

Household sponge

Scissors

Craft knife

Paper towels

Artist's brushes—one small and flat,
one small and round

Fine-tip black permanent marker

Wire cutters

*Patterns for this design are on page 138.*

### 1

With the fine-grit sandpaper, sand the rough edges smooth, removing any debris with a tack cloth.

### 2

To seal the wood, apply a coat of varnish to the top, sides, shelf, and legs of the table. Allow to dry.

### 3

Paint the table with two coats of light blue paint, allowing the first coat to dry thoroughly before applying the second one. Allow to dry.

### 4

Cut the household sponge into small pieces. Dip a piece of the sponge into the black paint and sponge the paint on the top and sides of the table. Apply pressure to the sponge as you work—you want the sponged areas to be dark. Allow to dry.

### 5

Position one lace place mat to cover the top, including the sides, of the table. Working a section at a time, lift the place mat and apply the decoupage medium to the tabletop with a foam brush. Then, lay that section of the place mat down onto the tabletop and decoupage medium. Smooth any wrinkles or bubbles from each section of the place mat as you work, also checking that the lace is adhering to the table's surface. Repeat this procedure until the top of the table is completely covered with lace.

### 6

Apply the decoupage medium to the sides of the table-top and smooth on the lace edges. For the corners, apply extra medium and smooth the lace under the edges of the top. Hold the lace in place for a few seconds until you're sure it will stay there.

### 7

To seal the lace in place, apply two coats of decoupage medium to the tabletop and its sides. Allow to dry.

### 8

From the second place mat, cut four lace shapes that will fit the front, sides, and bottom shelf of the table. Decoupage them as you did in Steps 5-7.

## 9

Using the heavyweight paper or cardstock, make two stencils from the flower-shaped motifs on page 138. Or make stencils of flower shapes of your choice, making one ¾" (2 cm) wide and the other 1"(2.5 cm) wide. Use a craft knife to cut out the shapes.

## 10

To stencil, lay the stencil on the surface, dip a piece of the household sponge in the paint, blotting off any excess paint on a paper towel, then apply the sponge to the stencil. Use the lavender paint on the larger flower stencil and periwinkle on the smaller one. Alternate them in an allover pattern on the smaller lace pieces and on the inside and outside of the legs and sides. If you choose, you may do the back. You may want to practice your stenciling technique on a scrap of paper before stenciling the table.

## 11

Trace or transfer the patterns for the cup, saucer, and three bonbons onto the muslin. Trace the outline of a teaspoon onto the muslin. Cut these shapes out.

## 12

To paint the saucer, use the flat brush to paint a periwinkle border, outlining it in white. Then paint a periwinkle circle in the center and outline it in white. Paint the rest of the saucer lavender. Using the round brush, make dots on the outer border.

**13**

To paint the cup, use the flat brush to paint the top and bottom of the cup light blue, then paint the bottom and handle periwinkle. Add lavender slashes to the handle and stencil or paint small lavender flowers to the bottom of the cup. Paint the coffee black with a white squiggle in the center.

**14**

For the spoon, paint it gray, then add white and black highlights. You may want to observe the real spoon to see how light affects the color of the metal.

**15**

To paint the bonbons, paint each bottom black and each top a different color—yellow-orange, pink, and light pink. Using the black marker, outline the edges. Paint white squiggly lines on top of each bonbon, and vertical white lines on each bottom.

**16**

Decide the placement of the appliques and glue them to the table. Place and

glue the saucer first. Next, glue the cup on it, placing the cup so it is to the side of the saucer. Place the spoon to rest on the saucer's edge. Arrange the three bonbons to the side, leaving space between them.

**17**

To make shadows around the appliques, mix a wash of black paint and water. Use a brush to apply the wash to the same sides of the appliqued objects. To show roundness and add depth, paint the wash on the sides of the cup and around the insides of the saucer. Allow to dry.

**18**

Apply two coats of varnish to the table, allowing the first coat to dry before applying the second one. Allow to dry.

**19**

Using a wire cutter, clip off the loops on the backs of the dome buttons. Using a strong adhesive, glue one button to the table front, and the other to the top of the bottom shelf.

# Fiesta Night Table

**T**his bright and festive night table is no sleeper. The colors alone will light up the darkest room, and the energetic pattern will make you want to dance with joy. Designer Shelley Lowell says her objective was to create a design that utilizes and plays off the structural elements of the furniture, specifically the knobs and drawers.

*Designer: Shelley Lowell*

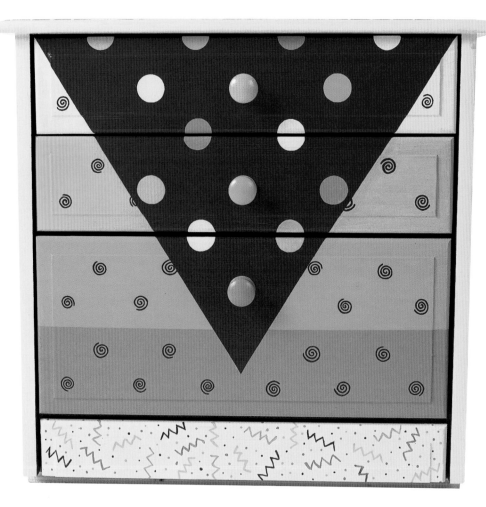

*actual size: 23$\frac{1}{2}$"w x 18-$\frac{1}{4}$"d x 22"h (59.5 x 46 x 56 cm)*

## Materials

Three-drawer chest

Wood filler

Gesso

Acrylic artist's paint in yellow, cobalt blue, orange, yellow, green, aqua, and white (optional)

Pastel pencil or chalk

Water-based polyurethane

## Tools

Ruler

Small hand or power drill (if needed)

Sandpaper in medium and fine grit

Tack cloth

Low-tack (blue) painter's masking tape

Paintbrushes in various sizes

Artist's brushes with both flat and round tips, including a small chisel brush (a brush with a triangular tip)

Tracing or transfer paper

Disposable brush

### 1

Because the symmetry of the design calls for the knobs to be at the same distance from the top of the drawers, you may need to reposition the knobs depending on the piece of furniture you're using. Since the bottom drawer of this chest is larger, only the bottom knob was moved. If you need to do this, first measure the distance between the top of the knob and the top of the drawer on the first or second drawer. Using that measurement, measure down from the top of the third drawer and mark the position for the new hole. With a small power or hand drill, drill the new hole. Then fill the old hole with wood filler.

### 2

Fill any holes, cracks, or uneven areas with wood filler. Remove excess, let dry, then sand the patches until smooth. Remove the knobs.

### 3

Sand the entire surface once with medium-grit sandpaper, then once again with fine-grit sandpaper. Wipe off all dust with a tack cloth (or use a vacuum cleaner).

### 4

Paint the entire table, including the drawer fronts, with gesso. When dry, sand with fine-grit sandpaper. Apply another coat of gesso and let dry. If there are still rough areas, lightly sand again. If needed, apply a third coat of gesso and lightly sand and clean before applying the paint.

### 5

Remove the drawers. Using the photograph as a guide, paint a base coat of yellow as indicated on all but the top drawer. Allow to dry.

### 6

Put the drawers back. To mark the lines for the large blue triangle on the front of the drawers, use chalk or a pastel pencil and draw a vertical line down the middle of the drawers through the knob holes. Using a ruler as a guide, draw the two sides of the triangle, slanting down from the top corners of the top drawer. Put the knob back on the first drawer, mark a circle around it, then remove it.

### 7

Using the masking tape, lay the tape along the side lines of the triangle drawn in Step 6. To seal the edges of the tape, apply a coat of yellow over the tape, bleeding the yellow into the yellow base coat. Allow to dry. Seal the opposite edge of the tape with the blue paint before painting the entire triangle blue except where the circle has been drawn. Allow to dry. (See the Tip below for using masking tape.)

### 8

With chalk or a pastel pencil, and using a knob as a template, draw the other circles as indicted in the photograph. Using either gesso or white acrylic paint, carefully paint these circles and allow to dry. (The gesso or white paint creates a base coat that helps prevent the darker blue from bleeding through the circles. If you were to paint the colors directly on the blue, you would need to recoat the circles several times to get clean, clear colors.) Using the photograph as a guide, paint the circles with the appropriate colors.

**9**

On the top two drawers, use the tape to mask off the blue areas. Seal the "triangle" edge of tape with blue and allow to dry. Seal the opposite edge of tape with gesso or white paint. Then, with the gesso or white paint, paint into the outer edges of the drawers. When dry, paint over the white areas on the top drawer with yellow, and the white areas on the middle drawer with orange.

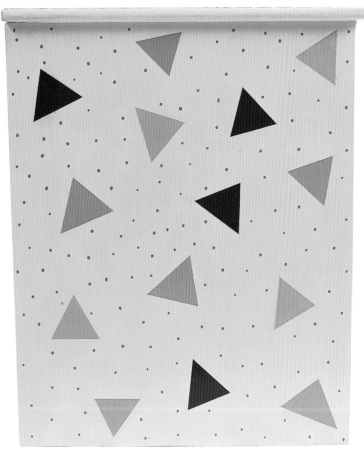

Side

**10**

On the bottom drawer, draw a line where the green and aqua will meet. Mask off one of the color areas. It doesn't matter which one you choose to do first—just remember to apply a coat of gesso or white paint before applying the final color coat. When the paint is dry, repeat the procedure by masking and painting the other color area. Using the photograph as your color guide, paint the knobs.

**11**

On the sides, use chalk or a pastel pencil to draw random triangles. Mask off the triangles with tape, sealing the edges with yellow paint. Allow to dry, then paint the triangles in the colors as indicated. (You don't need to paint the triangles white first as you did for the circles on the blue. Since the yellow is light in value, it's easy to cover and will not interfere with the clarity of the final colors.)

**12**

To make the small aqua dots, take an artist's brush and dip the tip of the handle lightly into the paint, which should be the consistency of cream. "Dot" the color onto the surface. Dip the tip in the color before making each dot.

**13**

After one side is done, you can randomly place the triangles and dots on the other side, following the same procedures. Or, trace and transfer (see page 15) the placement of the triangles and dots on the completed side to the other side before painting.

**14**

For the top, use the ruler and chalk or pastel pencil to measure and mark a frame around the edges. Then draw a square in each corner that is $\frac{1}{4}$" (.5 cm) bigger than your frame. For instance, if your frame is $1\frac{3}{4}$" (4.5 cm) wide, the square should be 2" (5 cm). Mask off this frame, including the corners of the square, seal the tape's edges with yellow, then paint. Allow to dry, then paint the center of the top blue.

**15**

Draw lines to divide the frame into bars. The width of the bars will be determined by the dimensions of the piece you're painting. The designer used a width of ⅜" (1 cm). Once the lines are drawn, mask off the yellow, sealing the edges with yellow, then paint the alternate bars green.

**16**

For the squares, find a bottle cap or jar cover that is about ½" (1.5 cm) less than the width of the square to use as a template. Center it in the square and trace its outline. Carefully paint the circle orange and the area outside the circle aqua.

**17**

To make the edge around the three sides of the frame, begin by measuring the width of the top, then divide that measurement in half. Lay tracing paper on the top, marking the halfway measurement. Then draw connecting lines like zigzags. Using transfer paper (see page 14), transfer these lines to the front and side of the top. Note: It may be easier for you to do this freehand.

**18**

Paint the aqua and orange areas first, leaving about ¹⁄₁₆" (.16 cm) between the yellow. When done, take a tiny chisel brush and paint over the yellow line. If you go out of the lines, you can always touch up with the final color.

**19**

For the bottom front, paint random orange, blue, green, and aqua zigzags. Then, using the tip of the brush's handle, make random dots of these same colors as you did in Step 13.

Top

**20**

Using the photograph as your guide, paint the knobs.

**21**

Allow the paint to dry. It's best to let the paint dry for at least 24 hours to allow it to cure properly. Wipe off any excess chalk.

**22**

After 24 hours, use a soft brush or disposable sponge brush to apply the polyurethane coating. Apply three coats for durability, allowing each coat to dry thoroughly before applying the next. Enjoy!

**TIP:** Proper use of masking tape will give you good clean edges and will prevent any paint from pulling up when you remove the tape. A good rule of thumb is to lay the tape, then seal one edge first with the color of paint that is under the tape. Allow to dry slightly (to touch). Then seal the other edge of the tape with the color of paint you'll be using in the adjoining area before painting. While this may seem more time consuming, it will actually save you time, since you'll have a cleaner edge that will take little or no retouching once you remove the tape.

# Chalkboard Dresser

**C**hildren will have a great time creating their own changeable decorations with a chalkboard dresser in their room. It's also a lifesaver for mom—she won't get angry when the kids decide to scribble on this furniture!

*Designer: Mary Devereaux*

## Materials

Five-drawer dresser

White all-purpose primer—or follow the chalkboard finish manufacturer's recommendations for suitable primer

Spray chalkboard finish in green

Semigloss acrylic paints in colors of your choice

Artist's acrylic paints in colors of your choice

Permanent opaque paint markers: fine-tip (used here—gold metallic and blue); medium fine- and broad-tip (used here—purple, crimson, yellow, and orange)

Water-based polyurethane

## Tools

2" (5 cm) disposable foam brushes

Fine-grit sandpaper

Tack cloth

Low-tack painter's masking tape

Artist's brushes

### 1
Remove the knobs and set aside.

### 2
To minimize the wood grain for a smooth chalkboard finish and to strengthen the surface of the wood, apply three coats of primer. Allow each coat to dry thoroughly. Sand between coats, removing any debris before applying the next coat.

*actual size: 25½"w x 15"d x 40¼"h (64.5 x 38 x 102 cm)*

**3**

Using the tape, mask off the areas where you do not want the chalkboard finish to go—you'll paint these later. Remember to include the smaller areas, such as the horizontal slats between the drawers and the edges of drawers.

**4**

Following the manufacturer's instructions for the chalkboard finish, apply at least three coats. Allow each coat to dry thoroughly, sanding lightly and removing all debris between the first and second coats. When the chalkboard paint is completely dry, remove the tape.

**5**

Use the bright acrylic paints or artist's colors to paint the base coat for the borders around the sides and the drawers of the dresser. The bright colors will enliven the flat green of the chalkboard surface. Note: For touch-ups, you might find it useful to purchase some of the opaque markers in colors to match the border colors. The markers are more convenient to use than an artist's brush and will make a smoother line for covering tiny mishaps.

**6**

While liquid acrylic colors were used to paint the borders on this piece, you can also use spray paint. To do this, use newspaper and masking tape to cover and protect the chalkboard surfaces before spraying the borders. If the chalkboard paint is marred by removing the masking tape, you can cover any small imperfections with design motifs or the opaque markers.

Top

**7**

Use the artist's brushes and paint, or opaque markers, to apply the design motifs to the borders. You may want to sketch ideas out beforehand. Try to carry the same theme for the decorations throughout. Choose motifs that can be easily repeated and can be adapted in size, such as geometrics, animals, toys, etc. You can mask off areas as you paint to ensure clean edges, or use a steady hand or a loose freehand to create your design. You can also stencil or sponge print your motifs. If you're working with a child to create the designs, remember the markers are permanent and will stain clothing, rugs, and walls.

**8**

Paint the knobs to match the borders, allow to dry, then coat them with the water-based polyurethane, allowing it to dry before reattaching the knobs.

**9**

Follow the manufacturer's instructions for preparing the chalkboard surface before use. A standard preparation is to use the side of a piece of calcium carbonate chalk to cover the entire chalkboard area. With a felt eraser, erase the chalk, and the surface is ready for use. Scribble away!

# Jelly Cabinet

**T**he bright splashes of random color create an artistic statement on this fanciful yet functional piece. To get the look, apply a colorful base coat, cover it with a coat of white, then strategically sand to reveal the colors underneath.

*Designer: Laurey-Faye Long*

## Materials

Jelly cabinet

Acrylic artist's colors—small amounts in bright colors

Dark acrylic paint in a color of your choice

White acrylic paint

Pack of multi-color construction paper

White glue

Clear matte spray acrylic sealer or acrylic varnish

## Tools

2" (5 cm) paintbrush

4" (10 cm) paintbrush

Dust mask

Electric sander with #120 sandpaper

Tack cloth or rags

#400 sandpaper

Scissors

### 1

Prepare the cabinet for painting by removing the door. Unscrew all the hardware and set it aside.

### 2

Randomly paint the exterior surfaces, including the door, with wild streaks of bright colors, making sure to apply the colors to the edges and corners as well. Allow to dry.

### 3

Paint the interior of the cabinet and the interior surface of the door with the dark solid color. Allow to dry.

### 4

Once the bright colors are dry, paint all exterior surfaces white. Allow this last white coat to dry thoroughly—the desired effect created in the following step will not succeed if you work when the paint is damp.

### 5

Using the electric sander and the #120 sandpaper, sand off portions of the white coat to allow the base colors to show through. Wear the dust mask to protect yourself from breathing sawdust and small particles of paint as you work. To get the look you want, try sand-

ing a test patch in an inconspicuous area first, experimenting with varying pressures. You may occasionally sand to bare wood. This is fine—just think of the wood as another color that will show through.

### 6

Continue to sand the entire exterior of the cabinet. To get a tight line of revealed color at the edges and corners, hold the sander at a right angles to them. Note: On this cabinet, the white paint was almost totally sanded from the top, while a good portion of the white was left on the body of the piece. Decide beforehand how you want your piece to look, so you can plan where you'll sand for the effect you want.

### 7

Stop sanding with the electric sander when you are pleased with the balance of bright colors and white areas. Remove any debris using a tack cloth or damp rag.

### 8

Using the #400 sandpaper, hand sand the interior of the cabinet and the door, removing any debris.

### 9

Apply clear matte acrylic spray sealer to the interior and exterior. To avoid drips, it's always best to apply two light coats rather than one heavy one, allowing the first coat to dry before applying the second. You may also use matte acrylic varnish in a can and brush it on.

### 10

Once the sealer has dried, hand sand the exterior of the cabinet with #400 sandpaper, remove any debris, and apply a second coat of sealer or varnish.

### 11

The interior of the cabinet door was decorated with cut construction paper. To do this, apply the designs of your choice with white glue, smoothing the paper tightly to the wood. When the glue is dry, spray the door and the cutouts with acrylic sealant. This step is optional—you may decide to keep the interior of the door a solid color.

*actual size: 19¹/₂"w x 12¹/₂"d x 47¹/₂"h (49.5 x 31.5 x 120 cm)*

# Rustic "Punched Tin" Cabinet

**L**ook again—if you thought the doors were made from punched tin! They're actually crafted from the skillful application of silver and black paint to create the illusion of this traditional country technique.

*Designer: Lindsey Morgan*

*actual size: 27"w x 18"d x 34½"h*
*(68.5 x 45.5 x 87.5 cm)*

## Materials

Cabinet

Water-based primer

Spray stain blocker

Wood filler

Latex semigloss paint in orange and red

Silver spray paint

Black acrylic craft paint

Latex polyurethane

## Tools

3" (7.5 cm) paintbrush

Sandpaper in medium and fine grit

Tack cloth or rags

Coarse-grit sandpaper, made for paint and varnish removal

Low-tack painter's masking tape

Pencil

Small artist's brush

### 1

Take off the doors and remove the hardware, including the knobs.

### 2

Spray the knots with the stain blocker. Remember to take special care to seal the knots when working in pine so the wood's tannin will not eventually bleed through the paint (see page 14). Allow the stain blocker to dry, then prime the entire piece with the water-based primer.

### 3

Use wood filler to fill any holes or imperfections and allow to dry. Sand the patches smooth with medium-grit sandpaper, removing any debris with a tack cloth.

### 4

For the base coat, paint the piece with the orange paint and allow to dry. Then sand the entire piece with fine-grit sandpaper, remove any debris, and paint again. Allow the paint to dry. Do not paint the inside panels of the doors with the orange paint—if some of it gets on them, however, don't worry about it.

### 5

Over this orange base coat, paint the piece red. Just as in Step 4, apply one coat, allow it to dry, sand, remove debris, then paint again.

### 6

When the paint is dry, use the coarse sandpaper to lightly sand the piece. Apply more pressure with the sandpaper around the edges of the piece and around the handle areas until some of the orange paint shows through. Be careful not to sand too hard, you don't want to sand down to the primer coat or the bare wood.

### 7

Using the masking tape, tape off the red painted edges of the door panels, making sure you seal the edges of the tape well. Spray the panels with the silver paint and allow to dry. Sand lightly with fine paper, and spray again. (To avoid drips, it's always best to apply two light coats rather than one heavy one.) When the paint is dry, remove the tape.

## 8

Using the pencil, lightly sketch the stars on the silver panels. Dip the tip of the handle of the small artist's brush in black craft paint and "punch the holes" by dotting the paint to the outline of the stars. Fill in some areas with "holes" if desired. Allow the paint to dry.

## 9

Apply two coats of polyurethane to the red/orange sections of the piece, sanding lightly between coats. Replace the hardware on the doors, and reattach the doors to the cabinet.

**TIPS:** Knots bleeding through the paint will add a primitive look that can add to the overall rustic appearance of the piece. If you want this to happen, do not apply the stain blocker, as described in Step 2, to the base of the piece. (You'll always need to block the knots in the areas you'll be painting silver.)

When you're sanding the edges and the corners of the piece to get to the orange base coat, it's hard to keep from sanding through to the primer. To help, once you've applied the base coat and have allowed it to dry, lightly rub the edges and corners with a white candle before applying the red paint.

# Terra-Cotta and Verdigris Finish Cart

**T**exture adds interest to this versatile cart which can be used in a kitchen for extra storage, or in a den as a television stand. For the top, spattering mineral spirits on wet latex creates an interesting, random pattern that enhances the metallic verdigris illusion.

*Designer: Kevin Fulford*

## Materials

| |
|---|
| Cart |
| Wood filler |
| All-purpose primer |
| Latex paint, satin-finish in creamy yellow, dark gray-blue (verdigris), and brown |
| Crackle medium |
| Oil glaze |
| Linseed oil |
| Odorless paint thinner |
| Mixing containers |
| Artist's oil colors in raw sienna and burnt umber |
| Mineral spirits |
| Clear acrylic varnish |

## Tools

| |
|---|
| Fine-grit sandpaper |
| Rags |
| Tack cloth |
| 2" or 3" (5 or 7.5 cm) paint brushes |
| 2" (5 cm) bristle brush |
| Sea sponge |
| 2" (5 cm) round, long-haired bristle brush (fitch) |
| Artist's flat lining brush |
| Ruler |
| Pencil |

*actual size: 27"w x 18"d x 34½"h*
*(68.5 x 45.5 x 87.5 cm)*

### 1

Fill any imperfections in the wood with wood filler, allow to dry, then sand the patches smooth with fine-grit sandpaper. Sand the entire piece lightly with fine-grit sandpaper, removing any debris with a tack cloth or damp rag.

### 2

Seal any knots until they no longer bleed through the primer-sealer or shellac. Apply a coat of all-purpose primer and allow to dry.

**3**

Apply a base coat to the bottom of the stand (exclude the top) using the satin-finish creamy yellow latex, and allow to dry.

**4**

Following the manufacturer's instructions, apply the crackle medium in random patches to the sides and doors of the piece.

**5**

Apply a second coat of the satin-finish creamy yellow latex.

**6**

Thin the oil glaze with a small amount of linseed oil. Take one part of this thinned glaze and mix it with one part odorless paint thinner. Tint with the raw sienna and burnt umber until you have a terra-cotta color.

Top

**7**

Working one section at a time, apply the terra-cotta glaze. Use a clean rag to dab at the wet glaze to create a mottled effect, then use a bristle brush to lightly blend these contrasting light and dark areas together. For added toning as you continue to rag and blend, occasionally and randomly introduce small amounts of raw sienna and burnt umber directly from the tubes to the terra-cotta glaze. Allow the glaze to dry.

**8**

Varnish with an acrylic clear coat.

**9**

To make the verdigris finish on the top, apply the dark gray-blue latex with a damp natural sponge. Next, sponge on the brown latex paint sparingly as an accent. Allow to dry.

**10**

Varnish with an acrylic clear coat.

**11**

Thin some of the gray-blue paint with water. Brush the top of the cart with water, then brush on the thinned latex. Working while the latex is wet, take the round brush (fitch), dip it in mineral spirits, and use it to spatter (spritz) the mineral spirits randomly on the latex. You want the paint and mineral spirits to separate, creating a beading effect. If the finish blurs, wipe off and start again, using less water. If the spattering still doesn't result in the desired effect, wipe off and try using more water. Allow to dry. You may want to try a sample piece first to get the right proportions of water to paint and mineral spirits (and to practice your spattering).

**12**

When dry, varnish with an acrylic clear coat.

**13**

For added visual interest, use a ruler as a guide to lay out a diamond pattern on the front and sides, marking it lightly with a pencil. Using the flat lining brush, apply the terra-cotta glaze over the pencil lines.

# Optical Illusion Three-Drawer Chest

**P**lay with the illusion of a fanciful bird-filled window. Your guests will appreciate the touch of humor, and you'll appreciate how easy it is to decorate this simple chest.

*Designer: Erec Trey Weekes*

*actual size:*
*23½"w x 18¼"d x 22"h*
*(59.5 x 46 x 56 cm)*

## Materials

Three-drawer chest

Latex semigloss enamel in white, blue, pink, red, black, brown, dark green, and medium green

Water-based varnish or polyurethane in a matte finish

## Tools

Fine-grit sandpaper

Tack cloth

2" (5 cm) angled paintbrush

Ruler

Pencil

Low-tack masking tape

Two round artist's brushes, large and medium

*Patterns for this design are on page 139.*

**1**

Remove the knobs from the drawers. Lightly sand the chest, using the fine-grit sandpaper, and remove any debris with the tack cloth.

**2**

Apply one coat of white paint as the primer and allow to dry. Apply a second coat of white paint as the base coat and allow to dry.

**3**

With the photograph as your visual guide, use the ruler and pencil to measure and mark the lines for the "window frame" on the drawers. Use the shape of the drawers to help in creating the illusion.

**4**

Copy the patterns on pages 139, enlarging if necessary. Using the transfer or tracing paper, transfer the motifs to the chest. (Instructions for transferring are on pages 14-15.)

**5**

Paint the blue background first and allow to dry.

**6**

Using the low-tack masking tape, mask the blue areas, sealing the edges well to avoid any paint from

seeping underneath. Paint the "window frames" pink and allow to dry.

**7**

Mix some of the pink paint with a small amount of the white paint to make a slightly

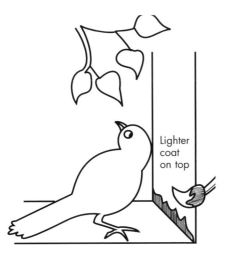

lighter hue of pink. Repaint the "window frame" with the lighter pink, stopping 1/16" (.16 cm) from the corners—exposing the darker pink will help with the perspective.

**8**

For the branch, paint it once with black and allow to dry. Apply a coat of brown over the black, leaving a 1/8 to 1/4" (.3 to .5 cm) edge of black unpainted.

**9**

Paint the leaves dark green and allow to dry. Apply a coat of medium green over the dark green, leaving a 1/8 to 1/4" (.3 to .5 cm) edge of dark green unpainted.

**10**

Paint the birds a solid color, allowing the whites of their eyes to show.

**11**

Transfer and paint images on the sides and top. You

Left Side

can place them as directed on page 139—or where you like.

**12**

Don't forget to paint the knobs! Use them as part of the design. Here they're painted to look like interesting bits of fruit that are attracting the birds to the window.

**13**

Apply two coats of varnish or polyurethane to the chest, including the knobs. Allow the first coat to dry completely before applying the second one. When dry, replace the knobs.

# Antiqued Tall Boy

**M**ake the new look instantly old with this easy antiquing technique. The use of opaque latex paint imitates the look of casein paint (also known as milk paint, since its base was made from milk) which was used in colonial America and by the Shakers.

*Designer: Traci Dee Neil-Taylor*

*actual size: 21¼"w x 17"d x 53¼"h*
*(54 x 43 x 135 cm)*

## Materials

| |
|---|
| Tall boy dresser |
| Opaque flat latex paint in light green and white |
| Water-based crackle glaze medium |
| Water-based varnish in a matte finish |

## Tools

| |
|---|
| Medium-grit sandpaper |
| Tack cloth |
| Newspapers |
| 2" and 3" (5 and 7.5 cm) paintbrushes |

### 1

Lay newspapers on the floor to protect it from any spills or drips.

### 2

Lightly sand the dresser with medium-grit sandpaper. You don't want a totally smooth surface—this piece will look older if the wood is roughed up a bit. Remove any debris with the tack cloth.

### 3

Apply the green base coat directly to the wood and allow to dry for 24 hours. If you prefer, you can prime the wood with all-purpose primer-sealer before applying the base coat, allowing the primer to dry thoroughly before applying the paint.

### 4

Since you want some of the base coat to show through, decide beforehand which areas of the piece will have the crackled effect. Generously apply the crackle glaze medium on these areas, and allow to dry for at least 2 hours.

### 5

Working in one direction, apply the white top coat to the areas that have the crackle medium. Don't paint over your strokes—going back and forth over the crackle medium will minimize the results. Long strokes will produce long crackles, while short strokes produce short crackles. Allow the top coat to dry.

Note: If your base coat is significantly darker than your top coat, the crackles will show dark veins through the top coat. Since the base and top coats are close in color value on this piece, they produce a more subtle effect.

### 6

A apply a coat of matte-finish water-based varnish.

**TIP:** Depending on the amount of antiquing desired, apply more crackle medium for a more distressed look. Another variation is to use the medium-grit sandpaper to sand down to the wood in certain areas, such as on the edges of the body of the piece and on the edges of the drawer fronts.

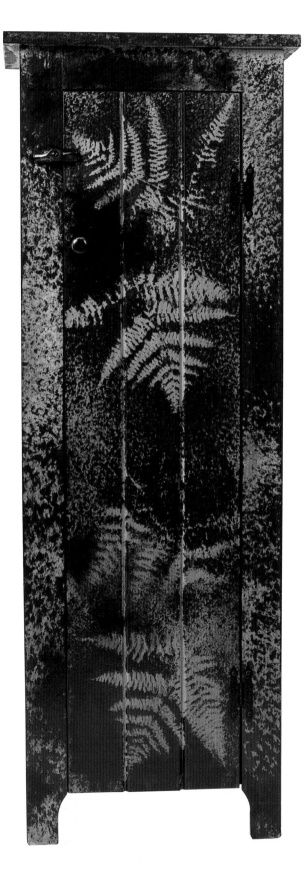

# Stippled Fern Jelly Cupboard

**E**ven if you live in the heart of the city, evoke thoughts of a refreshing mountain lodge with this cupboard. The use of the bold fern motif with the free-spirited stippling technique creates an instant rustic look.

*Designer: Lisa Sanders*

## Materials

Jelly cupboard

Oil-based paint, 1 pint (.5 L) each in black and brown

Small plastic container with an airtight lid

Several fern fronds

Oil-based wood stain, 1 pint (.5 L) in pecan

Oil-based polyurethane, 1 pint (.5 L)

*actual size: 18"w x 10¾"d x 48"h (45.5 x 27.5 x 122 cm)*

## Tools

| |
|---|
| Fine-grit sandpaper |
| Tack cloth |
| Rags or paper towels |
| Dropcloth |
| Screwdriver |
| Rubber gloves |
| Stir stick |
| Paint tray |
| Stippling brush* |
| 2" (5 cm) paintbrush |

*A stippling brush is a round brush with a flat-end made of natural hair, most commonly from badger.

**1**

Check the surface of the cupboard for any rough spots and sand them smooth with fine-grit sandpaper. Use a tack cloth or damp rag to remove any dust and dirt.

**2**

Spread the drop cloth and set the cupboard on it. Remove all hardware such as hinges, handles, or door fastener. Lay the door to the side.

**3**

Put on the rubber gloves. Mix the black and the brown paint together in the small plastic container, stirring well. Pour the paint into the paint tray.

**4**

Starting with the door, place a fern leaf near the top of the door and hold it in position with one hand. With the other hand, dip the stippling brush in the paint, then stipple all around the leaf with the black-brown paint. If needed, move your hand to finish stippling around the entire leaf. To stipple, dab the brush as you work—do not drag it. You may want to practice this technique on paper first.

**5**

Reposition the fern leaf on another part of the door (or use a new leaf if you have several) and repeat the stippling, dipping the brush in the paint as necessary. When you've finished stippling the door, repeat the process on the body of the cupboard starting with the top then on each of the sides. As you work, space the leaves randomly.

**6**

Set the ferns aside. Using only the stippling brush, continue to stipple the front frame and inside shelf edges. Let the paint dry overnight. Keep the remaining paint in the container and cover with the airtight lid.

**7**

Using the black-brown paint and the 2" (5 cm) brush, paint any areas of the cupboard that are unpainted. Let the paint dry.

**8**

Using a rag, apply the pecan stain to the cupboard everywhere you've stippled. Let it dry, then apply a second coat if necessary. If the door handle and door closure that you removed are wood, stain them also. Let the stain dry according to the manufacturer's instructions.

**9**

Apply a coat of polyurethane to the entire cupboard, including the door handle and closure. Let it dry, then apply a second coat.

**10**

Reassemble the cupboard by reattaching the hinges and door, door handle, and door closure.

# Benches & Stools

# Plaid Footstool

**P**aint an upholstered look with this faux plaid. Don't worry about a steady hand. The slightly wavy lines and blended edges create an authentic woven effect.

*Designer: Esther Doyle*

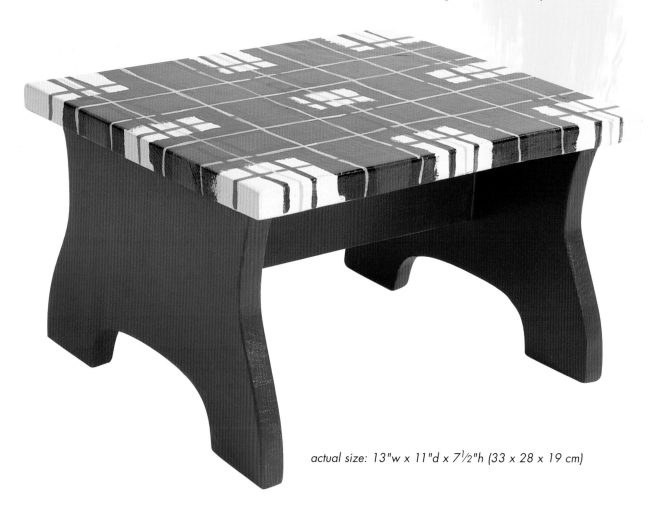

*actual size: 13"w x 11"d x 7½"h (33 x 28 x 19 cm)*

## Materials

Unfinished footstool

All-purpose wood sealer

Artist's acrylic paint, 2 oz. (60 mL) each, in soft white, alizarine crimson, cadmium red medium, Turner's yellow, cobalt blue, and Hooker's green

Low-lustre acrylic varnish

## Tools

Extra fine-grit sandpaper

2" (5 cm) paintbrush

Disposable plastic plates

1" (2.5 cm) and 3" (7.5 cm) paint rollers

#2 artist's liner brush

### 1
Sand the stool until smooth and no rough edges remain. Wipe off the dust with a damp, not wet, cloth. Allow to dry.

### 2
Mix equal parts of the wood sealer and the alizarine crimson. Coat the sides and underside of the stool. You may need an additional one to two coats to achieve an opaque look. *Do not mix any additional coats with the sealer.*

### 3
Mix equal parts of the wood sealer with the soft white. Use this to coat the top of the stool and the top's edges. You may need an additional one to two coats to achieve an opaque look. *Do not mix any additional coats with the sealer.*

### 4
Put some of the Hooker's green on a disposable plastic plate. With the 3" (7.5 cm) roller, pick up an even coat of the green. Roll two stripes, evenly spaced, across the stool from the top to the bottom (vertically). Then roll two stripes, evenly spaced, across the stool from side to side (horizontally). You will have four stripes of green. Using the roller, extend the edges of all four stripes onto the edges of the top. Allow to dry.

### 5
Put some of the alizarine crimson on a clean disposable plate. With the 1" (2.5 cm) roller, pick up an even coat of the crimson. Roll stripes down the center of each of the four green stripes. Allow to dry.

### 6
Slightly thin some of the yellow paint with water. Using the #2 liner brush, paint a narrow stripe on either side of the crimson stripes. Be sure to stay within the green vertical and horizontal stripes. Allow to dry.

### 7
Slightly thin some of the cadmium red medium paint with water. Using the #2 liner brush, paint narrow stripes of red horizontally all the way across the stool through all the white areas. Do not paint any vertical red stripes. Allow to dry.

### 8
Slightly thin some of the cobalt blue paint with water. Paint two narrow stripes vertically, positioned approximately 1" (2.5 cm) apart, through all the white areas. Allow to dry.

### 9
Using the #2 liner brush and the yellow paint, paint narrow stripes vertically from top to bottom between each pair of blue stripes. Allow to dry.

### 10
To create the woven look on the narrow stripes, paint over every other narrow line with the appropriate color. Allow to dry.

### 11
To seal and protect, paint the entire piece with low-lustre acrylic varnish.

# Jewel Stool

**W**ith fabric and fringe, jewels and wire, designer Maureen Donahue has shown how even the humblest piece of furniture can be transformed into a one-of-a-kind conversation piece.

*Designer: Maureen Donahue*

## Materials

| |
|---|
| Stool |
| Purple spray paint |
| Copper tubing, 84" (2.2 m) |
| Four electric wire fasteners |
| 4" (10 cm) upholstery foam, 14" (35.5 cm) square |
| Fine-point permanent marker |
| Fabric, size 24 x 50" (61 x 127 cm) |
| Self-covering button, 1½" (4 cm) |
| String |
| 4" (10 cm) bullion fringe, 48" (122 cm) |
| Jewels |
| Slider feet, for protecting the floor |

*actual size: 14" diameter x 27"h (35.5 x 68.5 cm)*

## Tools

| |
|---|
| Drill with 1" (2.5 cm) bit |
| Sandpaper in fine and extra fine grit |
| Hammer |
| Electric knife |
| Glue gun and glue sticks |
| Clamps |
| Staple gun |

### 1

Find the center of the seat. Use the drill to make a 1" (2.5 cm) hole. Using the fine-grit sandpaper, sand the stool and remove any debris.

### 2

Spray paint all but the top of the stool. After the first coat dries, sand with the extra fine-grit sandpaper and remove any debris. Apply a second coat of spray paint.

### 3

Cut the length of wire tubing in half. Using the hammer and a wire fastener, attach an end of one piece of copper tubing underneath the stool on the inside of a leg. Wrap the copper around the leg, continuing down until all of the tubing is used. Find a place on the inside of the leg where the tubing ends and attach another wire fastener to hold the tubing close to the leg. Do the same on the opposite leg.

### 4

Turn the stool upside down on the piece of foam. Trace the outline of the seat using the fine-point marker. Using the electric knife, cut out the foam holding the knife straight up and down.

### 4

Using the glue gun, glue the foam to the seat—being sure to include the outer edges. With the electric knife, cut a funnel-shaped hole in the center of the foam circle that corresponds to the 1" (2.5 cm) drilled hole.

The top of the funnel-shaped hole should be about 4" (10 cm) in diameter.

### 6

To make the rounded edge, measure and draw a line 1" (2.5 cm) down from the top of the foam all the way around. Using the glue gun, run a bead of glue on the line for a few inches, then pinch the top edge of the foam to the 1" (2.5 cm) line. Use small clamps to hold the foam in this position until the glue dries, then remove the clamps and continue working your way around the foam by gluing and clamping a few inches at a time.

### 7

Working around the seat, staple the fabric to the bottom of the seat approximately 1" (2.5 cm) in from the edge. To prevent raw edges, overlap and turn the fabric under when you get to where you started.

### 8

Pull the fabric up tightly and insert the ends through the funnel-shaped hole in the foam and the 1" (2.5 cm) hole you drilled in the seat. Turn the stool over on a clean surface and staple the ends of the fabric close to the hole in the seat.

### 9

Cover the button using a scrap of fabric. Tie an 8" (20.5 cm) piece of string onto the buttonhole. Pull the string through the hole in the seat and staple the string to the bottom of the seat to anchor the button.

### 10

Apply the bullion fringe by anchoring the first section with a staple to the edge of the seat. Using the glue gun, glue the fringe around the seat. When you get to the point where you started attaching the fringe, overlap the fringe slightly to cover the staple and turn the edge of the fringe under approximately $1/4$" (.5 cm) so that no raw edges show.

### 11

Using the glue gun, attach the jewels to the legs that aren't wrapped with copper. Attach the slider feet to the bottom of the legs.

# Flowered Bar Stool

**U**se this stool at your breakfast bar, and you'll be greeted with a fresh and vibrant bouquet of flowers every morning. You can also use this as a small and colorful table anywhere in your house to give dark spaces a fresh and cheery lift.

*Designer: Molly Tilden Rousey*

*actual size: 13" in diameter x 24"h (33 x 61 cm)*

## Materials

| |
|---|
| 24" (61 cm) stool |
| Latex satin-finish paint, 1 quart (1 L) each, in pink, red, black, light yellow, light green, white, aqua green, and light blue |
| Carbon transfer paper |
| 1 quart (1 L) of high-gloss polyurethane |

## Tools

| |
|---|
| 1" (2.5 cm) masking tape |
| 2" (5 cm) paintbrush |
| 1" (2.5 cm) paintbrush |
| Artist's fine-tip detail brush |

*Patterns for this design are on page 140.*

**1**

Paint the top and underside of the seat with two coats of aqua green. Note: For this step, and for all steps calling for two coats of paint, always allow the first coat to dry thoroughly before applying the second one.

**2**

Paint the legs red, applying two coats.

**3**

Using aqua green and yellow, paint the rungs, alternating the two colors. Apply two coats.

**4**

Paint the edges of the seat white, applying two coats.

**5**

When the white paint is dry, use the 1" (2.5 cm) masking tape to space strips of tape 1" (2.5 cm) apart on the white edges of the seat. Seal the edges of the tape well so the paint won't bleed underneath.

**6**

Using black paint, paint between the pieces of tape, allowing the paint to dry before removing the tape.

**7**

Use carbon paper to transfer the patterns for the flower, leaves, circle, and butterfly onto the stool. (See pages 14-15 for transfer instructions.) Paint inside the outlines of each shape with one coat of white paint.

**8**

When the white paint is dry, go back and paint each motif. Using the photograph as a visual guide, paint the butterfly yellow, the rose pink, the circles pink, the three-pointed flower light blue, and the vines and leaves light green.

**9**

When the paint is completely dry, use the black paint and the fine-tip brush to outline and detail each motif, following their patterns for the detail placement.

**10**

When the black paint is dry, use the fine-tip brush and white paint to make light and suggestive strokes for highlighting the details of each motif—do not use any solid lines. Using the same brush and paint, make short brush strokes along the rungs of the stool.

**11**

Allow the paint to dry for 24 hours before applying two to three coats of polyurethane for the finish. Allow each coat of polyurethane to dry thoroughly before applying the next one.

# Photo-Memory Footstool

**T**his unique photo-transfer process helps you to preserve your memories in a distinctively creative way. Present this furniture to family and friends as a way to capture treasured memories in a most useful (and comfortable) manner.

*Designer: Laurey-Faye Long*

*actual size: 13¹/₂" in diameter x 12¹/₄"h*
*(34 x 30.5 cm)*

## Materials

Stool

_____ paints in colors of your choice

_____ for top surface

_____ hotographs

_____ n

_____

_____

_____ ;

_____ rush

_____ f your choice and

_____ water. Give the top
_____ at of this thinned

_____ r and remove
_____ .

_____ edium to heavy
layers of acrylic medium, allowing each coat to dry
thoroughly before applying the next one.

### 5
When the acrylic medium is completely dry, soak the
color copies in water for 12 hours.

### 6
Remove the color copies from the water. Place them
face down on a smooth surface and gently rub away
all the white paper. The photo image will remain on
the acrylic medium. The front of the image will appear
milky, but as it dries, this white haze will disappear.
Allow to dry.

### 7
Brush the backs of the now-transparent copies with
acrylic medium. Transfer them to the painted stool top,
smoothing them as you lay them in position. Allow the
acrylic medium to dry.

### 8
Embellish the photo transfers with colored-pencil frames
and titles.

### 9
For a protective finish, apply two heavy coats of
acrylic medium to the entire top surface of the footstool. Allow each coat to dry thoroughly.

# Painted Mosaic Stool

If you want to make a mosaic, but don't know where to begin, try painting one first. This simple technique might fool your eye but not your artistic sensibilities. Once you feel confident with the procedure, try your own designs on a larger piece of furniture such as a table, dresser, or bookcase.

## Materials

Stool

All-purpose water-based primer

Spray stain blocker

Wood filler

Latex or acrylic craft paints in gray, bright blue, yellow, brown, orange, red, dark blue, black, and white

Water-based polyurethane

Oil-based stain in white

Oil-based polyurethane

Mineral spirits

## Tools

Sandpaper in medium and fine grit

Tack cloth or damp rag

2" (5 cm) paintbrush

Pencil or chalk

Small triangular cosmetic sponges

Craft knife or disposable snap-off blade

Small artist's brush

*Designer: Lindsey Morgan*

*actual size: 13$\frac{1}{2}$" in diameter x 24"h (34 x 61 cm)*

**1**

Fill any imperfections or nail holes with the wood filler, allow to dry, then sand the patches smooth.

**2**

Sand the entire stool with medium-grit sandpaper, using a tack cloth or damp rag to remove any debris. Allow to dry if necessary.

**3**

If there are any knots on the seat, spray them with the stain blocker and allow to dry.

**4**

Prime the seat with the all-purpose primer, allow to dry, then lightly sand with the medium-grit sandpaper. Remove any debris with a tack cloth or damp rag, and allow to dry if necessary.

**5**

Paint the seat with the gray paint and allow to dry. (Gray is the base coat that simulates the look of grout.) Sand the seat with the fine-grit sandpaper, removing any debris, and paint again. Allow to dry.

**6**

With a pencil, or chalk, lightly sketch the sun (or figure of your choice) on the seat.

**7**

Cut the cosmetic sponges in small pieces. Make some square, some triangular, and some irregular shapes.

**8**

Dip the edge of one of the sponges in the brown paint and lightly apply it to make the outline of the sun. Repeat this procedure using the black and red paints to outline the facial features and mouth. For the eyes, use a square sponge dipped in the darker blue paint.

**9**

With larger pieces of sponge, dab them into the paint and apply in a random fashion to fill in the sun, the rays, and the blue sky background. By mixing a little white paint with the bright blue background color, you can vary the color of the "tiles" to make them look

more realistic. Use smaller pieces of sponge to fill in the spaces between the larger "tiles." Allow paint to dry.

**10**

With a small artist's brush, use the gray "grout" color to touch up any smudges and allow to dry.

**11**

Apply two coats of polyurethane to the seat, allowing the first coat to dry thoroughly before applying the second one. Sand between coats with the fine-grit sandpaper.

**12**

Following the manufacturer's instructions, stain the legs and rungs of the stool with two coats of white stain. Lightly sand between coats with fine-grit sandpaper, removing any debris with a tack cloth or damp rag. Clean the brushes used for staining with mineral spirits.

**13**

Apply two coats of oil-based polyurethane to the legs, allowing each coat to dry completely before applying the second.

# Orange-Yellow Swirl Stool

The subtle coloration of this stool creates its own dramatic impact. By using colors within the same family that are close in value (light to dark), you can make a quiet but striking statement. Use this sunny palette, or experiment with colors to suit your own interior scheme.

*Designer: Mary Devereaux*

*actual size: 13¼" in diameter x 30"h (33.5 x 76 cm)*

## Materials

Stool

White all-purpose primer

Semigloss acrylic paints in three colors that are within the same color family and close in value (used here—pale orange, apricot, and medium orange)

Permanent opaque paint markers

Water-based polyurethane

## Tools

Fine-grit sandpaper

Tack cloth

2" (5 cm) disposable foam brushes

Pencil

½" (1.5 cm) flat artist's brush

**1**

Using the fine-grit sandpaper, lightly sand the entire surface, removing any debris with a tack cloth.

**2**

Using a 2" (5 cm) disposable brush and primer, prime the entire surface; allow to dry. Lightly sand the surface, removing any debris with a tack cloth, then apply a second coat of primer. If desired, apply a third coat of primer to protect the rungs from scuffing.

**3**

Paint the four legs in the lightest color. For the rungs, use varying hues. You can mix the lightest color with the darkest to create another color. Have fun experimenting!

**4**

For the seat, decide whether you want the swirl to go clockwise or counterclockwise. Using the photograph as a guide for sizing and placement, use a pencil to lighlty draw a simple swirl in the center of the seat.

You may want to draw the swirl on paper first, then transfer it to the seat. Paint this swirl the lightest color.

**5**

Using the ½" (1.5 cm) flat brush, begin painting the inner portion of the swirl with the darkest color. Change brushes and colors as the swirl expands, painting from the darkest to the lightest, blending the colors where they meet. Allow the paint to dry thoroughly, then use a gold metallic marker to outline the swirl.

**6**

Use a pencil to lightly draw the rays around the swirl, then trace over the lines with the gold metallic marker.

**7**

Once the design is dry, finish the piece by applying water-based polyurethane to all surfaces.

**TIPS:** When using oil-based markers over acrylic paint, thinner layers of paint are preferable to thick ones since they will prevent the marker paint from "ripping" through the acrylic.

Always use oil-based markers when using a water-based varnish or polyurethane. If you use water-based markers, the water in the water-based varnish or polyurethane will cause the markers to smear. Likewise, always use water-based markers when using an oil-based varnish or polyurethane.

# Weathered Fish Bench

**B**right colors, happy fish, and swirling waves make this a perfect bench for porch, poolside, or deck—even the shores of a tranquil garden pond. When you're done painting, give the bench an instant weathered look with a few easy passes of sandpaper strategically applied along the edges.

*Designer: Molly Tilden Rousey*

*actual size: 48"w x 12"d x 17"h
(122 x 30.5 x 43 cm)*

## Materials

Bench

Latex satin-finish paint, 1 quart (1 L) each, in royal blue, red, black, yellow, orange, white, and light blue

Carbon transfer paper

1 quart (1 L) of high-gloss polyurethane

## Tools

1" (2.5 cm) masking tape

2" (5 cm) paintbrush

1" (2.5 cm) paintbrush

Artist's fine-tip detail brush

Rubber "pointer" finger tip

Coarse-grit sandpaper, #60

Tack cloth

*Patterns for this design are on page, 141.*

**1**

Paint the underside of the bench with two coats of royal blue paint. Note: For this step, and for all steps calling for two coats of paint, always allow the first coat to dry thoroughly before applying the second coat.

**2**

Paint the top and outer two sides of the bench royal blue, applying two coats.

**3**

Paint the insides of the legs aqua green, applying two coats.

**4**

Paint both sides of the middle cross bar orange, applying two coats.

**5**

Paint the edges of the top of the bench and the top edge of the cross bar white, applying two coats.

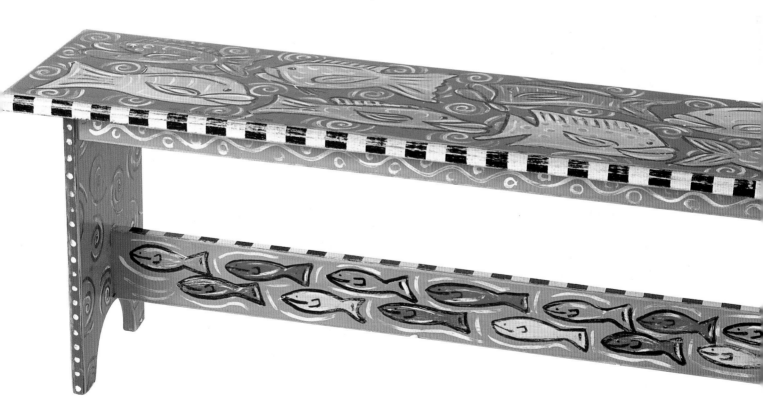

**6**

Paint the edges of the legs red, applying two coats.

**7**

Allow all paint to dry completely.

**8**

Use carbon paper to transfer the patterns of the big fish onto the top and sides of the bench. (See pages 14-15 for transfer instructions.) Refer to the photograph for placement. Paint inside the outlines of the fish with one coat of white paint.

**9**

Transfer the small fish patterns onto both sides of the cross bar. Use the white paint to paint within the outlines.

**10**

When the white paint is dry, paint each big fish using two colors of paint that you blend in the middle. Suggestions for color combinations are: yellow on top, orange on the bottom, blended in the middle; orange on the top, red on the bottom, blended in the middle; yellow on the top, light blue on the bottom, blended in the middle; yellow on the top, green on the bottom, blended in the middle.

**11**

When the paint is dry, detail each big fish with dots, stripes, and circles. To do this, dip the tip of the handle of the artist's brush in paint and apply randomly all over the fish to make the dots. (You can also use a rubber "pointer" fingertip dipped in paint to make the dots.) Use the fine-tip brush to make vertical stripes along fish bodies and to draw the circles. Detail yellow and orange fish with orange; orange and red fish with red; green and blue fish with green; and yellow and green fish with green.

**12**

Paint the small fish on the cross bar red, yellow, green, and royal blue, in alternating colors.

**13**

Use the fine-tip brush and the royal blue paint to make swirls on the insides of the bench legs.

**14**

Using the fine-tip brush and the green paint, make swirls between the fish on the blue background.

**15**

When the bench is dry, use black paint and the fine-tip brush to outline the big and little fish, following the detail lines of their patterns.

**16**

When the paint is completely dry, use the 1" (2.5 cm) masking tape to space small pieces of tape 1" (2.5 cm) apart on the white edges of the bench. Seal the edges of the tape well so the paint won't bleed underneath.

**17**

Using the black paint, paint between the pieces of tape, allowing the paint to dry before removing the tape.

**18**

Using the white paint and the fine-tip brush, highlight and outline the details on the fish. Use light, suggestive strokes—do not use any solid lines.

**19**

Use the same highlighting technique as in Step 18 on the swirls.

**20**

Using either the tip of the artist's brush handle or the "pointer" fingertip and the white paint, make evenly spaced dots on red edges of legs.

**21**

Allow the paint to dry for 24 hours.

**22**

For the weathered look, use the #60 coarse-grit sandpaper and sand all sides of the bench until you get the degree of weathered look you desire. Remove all debris with a tack cloth.

**23**

Apply two to three coats of polyurethane, allowing each coat to dry thoroughly before applying the next one.

# Bookcases

# Tropical Whimsy Bookcase/ Entertainment Unit

**C**reate a long-lasting and useful souvenir! Designer Gay Grimsley was inspired to make this tropical bookcase/entertainment unit after her trip to the Caribbean. You can easily adapt the idea to fit your own travel adventures—then anytime you see the piece, you'll be reminded of your wonderful time.

*Designer: Gay Grimsley*

## Materials

Bookcase/entertainment unit

All-purpose primer-sealer

Semigloss latex paint in medium green, dark green, medium yellow, medium terra-cotta, light terra-cotta, medium blue, and dark blue

Satin-finish polyurethane

Mineral spirits—if needed for clean up

## Tools

#220 sandpaper

Tack cloth

Rags

2" (5 cm) paintbrush

Low-tack painter's tape

Compressed sponge

Pencil

Craft knife

Disposable plastic plates

Paper towels

Small artist's brushes—one round, one flat

*Patterns for this design are on page 142.*

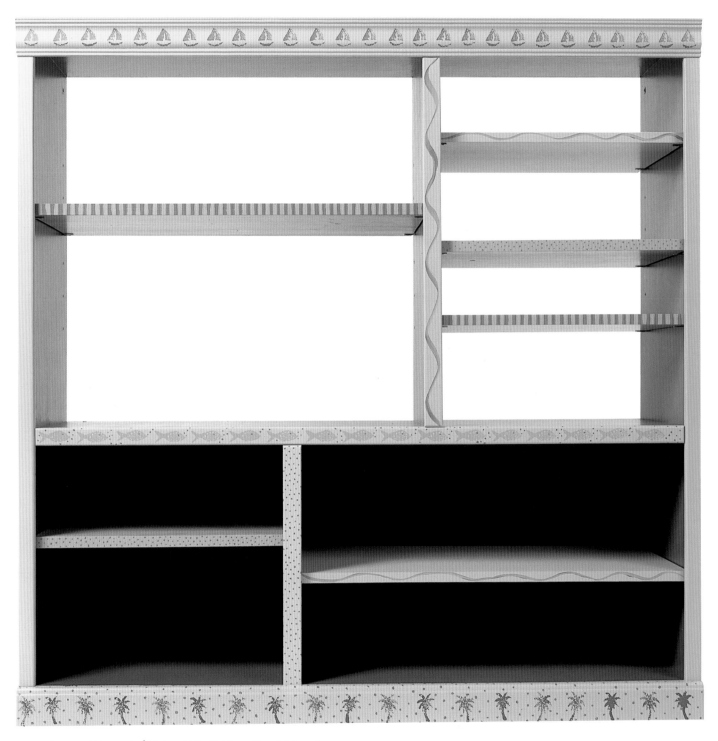

*actual size: 48"w x 16½"d x 48"h (122 x 42 x 122 cm)*

Side

**1**

With #220 sandpaper, sand the piece to smooth any rough edges or areas, removing any debris with a tack cloth or damp rag. Allow to dry if necessary.

**2**

With the primer-sealer, spot prime any knots in the wood to prevent them from bleeding through the paint. Allow to dry. Prime the entire piece, allow to dry, then sand again lightly with the #220 sandpaper, removing any debris.

**3**

Following the photograph as a visual guide, paint three coats each of the base colors on the selected areas of the piece. Allow each coat to dry thoroughly, sand lightly, and remove any debris before applying the next coat. When painting the border colors, use the painter's tape to mask off all adjoining colors, sealing the tape well to avoid any paint from seeping underneath. Allow all paint to dry completely.

**4**

Draw or transfer the simple shapes on the compressed sponge—fish, boat, palm tree, flower, and leaves. Cut out the shapes with a craft knife.

**5**

Immerse the cutout sponge shapes in water to expand, then squeeze out as much water as you can, leaving the sponge shapes slightly damp.

**6**

Put a small amount of paint on a disposable plastic plate. Dip the sponge shape you're working with in the paint and blot it out on paper towels to remove any excess paint.

**7**

Firmly press the sponge onto the piece, making sure the paint is evenly distributed. If it doesn't leave a good impression, wash it off and try again,

**8**

Repeat the process with each of the shapes in various colors.

**9**

Use a small round artist's brush for detailing to make the fish eyes, bubbles, flower stamen, and polka dots. Use a small flat artist's brush to make the waves and stripes on the shelves. allow to dry.

**10**

Apply three coats of polyurethane varnish, allowing each coat to dry completely before applying the next one.

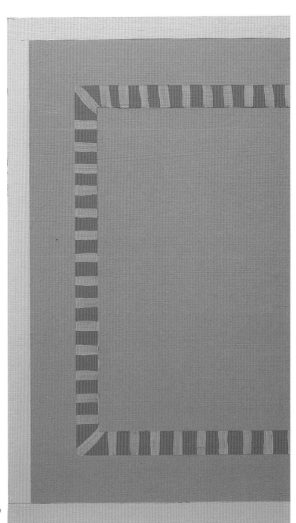

Top

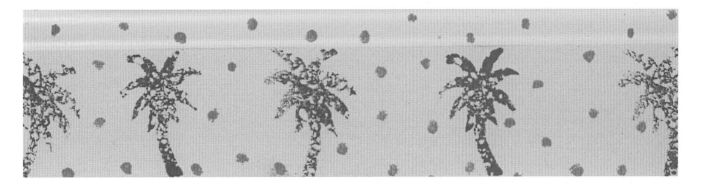

# Checkerboard-Bright Bookcase

*actual size: 36"w x 10"d x 36"h (91.5 x 25.5 x 91.5 cm)*

**A**dd a dash of color to your kitchen, jazz up a den, or brighten a child's room. The splash of red creates a vibrant, energetic look, while the surrounding colors harmonize to transform a plain bookcase into an eye-catching highlight.

*Designer: Esther Doyle*

## Materials

| |
|---|
| Bookcase |
| Latex primer |
| Latex semi-gloss enamel in dark royal blue, medium dark yellow, and deep red (choose colors of the same intensity) |
| Household sponge |
| Acrylic craft paint in lime green |
| Low-lustre acrylic varnish, or water-based polyurethane |

## Tools

| |
|---|
| Extra fine-grit sandpaper |
| ¾" (2 cm) masking tape |
| 2" (5 cm) angled paintbrush |
| Scissors |
| Small clamp or tweezers |
| #8 artist's brush for acrylic paints |

**1**

Sand the bookcase until it's smooth and no rough edges remain.

**2**

Wipe off the sanding dust with a damp cloth and allow the wood to dry.

**3**

Paint the bookcase with the latex primer. Allow to dry.

**4**

Paint the interior back with the red paint. You may need to apply several coats since you want a smooth, opaque color. Allow the paint to dry between coats, following the manufacturer's instructions.

**5**

With the ¾" (2 cm) masking tape, make a "frame" of tape around the outer edges of each side panel. As you tape, press the inside edges of the tape firmly to create a good seal that will keep paint from getting underneath.

**6**

Using the dark royal blue, paint the top of the bookcase, the bottom front panel, and the side panels inside the masking tape frame. To get a smooth, opaque look, you may need to apply two or three coats, allowing each coat to dry thoroughly before applying the next. You can speed the drying time between coats by using a hair dryer. However, you must allow the last coat to dry six to eight hours to prevent the paint from peeling away when you remove the masking tape. Once the paint is dry, carefully remove the masking tape.

**7**

When the blue paint is no longer tacky to the touch and you are certain it is thoroughly dry, use the masking tape to tape the inside edges of the blue sections of the side panels painted in Step 6. This will prevent the paint you are about to apply from bleeding into the blue, providing a nice "hard edge" for your border of yellow. Press the edges of the tape firmly to provide a good seal.

**8**

Using the medium dark yellow, paint the inside side panels and shelves. Paint the wood around the masked edges of the blue side panels, then paint the edges of the wood around the front of the bookcase, including the front edges of the shelves. Allow to dry. You may need to apply two coats, allowing each coat to dry thoroughly before applying the next.

**9**

Cut the kitchen sponge into a ⅜" (1 cm) square.

**10**

Using a small clamp or tweezers, dip the sponge square into a puddle of the lime green acrylic craft paint. Staggering the sponge printing in order to create a checkerboard effect, press the paint-coated sponge evenly to the yellow front edges of the shelves, the front edges around the bookcase, and the frame around the blue side panels. You may want to practice this technique by sponge printing on a piece of paper first.

**11**

To make the flowers, begin by making the dots that will become the center of each motif. Do this by dipping the wooden tip of the artist's brush ⅛" (.3 cm) into the yellow paint, then touch the paint-covered tip to the surface at the desired position. To ensure that the dots are the same size and color, reload the tip with paint after making each dot. Place the dots as follows: on the top, one in each corner and one at the center front and center back; on the sides, one in each corner of the blue panels, and one at the center front and center back of the long sides; on the bottom front panel, one at each lower corner and one in the center.

## 12

To make the teardrop petals around the dots, first dip the bristles of the #8 artist's brush in the lime green acrylic craft paint. Holding the end of the brush straight up, press the bristles down approximately 1" (2.5 cm) from a dot while slowly pulling toward the dot, releasing the pressure on the brush as you move closer to the dot. You may want to practice this on

paper first. Make three teardrops around each corner dot, and four teardrops around the remaining dots, spacing each teardrop evenly.

## 13

Allow all paint to dry thoroughly, preferably overnight. To protect the surface, finish the entire surface with low-lustre acrylic varnish or water-based polyurethane.

# Copper-trimmed Bookcase

**T**ry an updated country look! The warm glint of the copper trim complements the soft, mellow green of this bookcase. By using a rub-in stain, you can create a sheer color that highlights the grain and allows the wood to show through.

*Designer: Traci Dee Neil-Taylor*

*actual size: 17$\frac{1}{2}$"w x 9$\frac{1}{2}$"d x 60"h*
*(44.5 x 24 x 152 cm)*

## Materials

| |
|---|
| Bookshelf |
| Green wood stain (rub-in) |
| Polyurethane in a matte finish |
| Copper flashing, available at hardware stores |
| Copper nails |

## Tools

| |
|---|
| Old newspapers |
| Fine-grit sandpaper |
| Tack cloth |
| Lint-free rags |
| Protective work gloves |
| Metal shears (tin snips) |
| Drill with a 1/16" (.16 cm) bit |
| Hammer |

**1**

Lay newspapers on the floor to protect it from any spills or drips.

**2**

Sand the bookcase, using fine-grit sandpaper, removing any debris with the tack cloth.

**3**

Use a rag to apply the rub-in stain, following the manufacturer's instructions. Note: Using rub-in stain gives the wood a more distressed look than you'd get with a brush-on stain—just the right look for this piece. After applying the stain, allow to dry for 24 hours.

**4**

To seal the stain, apply a coat of matte-finish polyurethane and allow to dry.

**5**

Wearing the protective work gloves, use the tin snips to cut the desired designs for the shelf and side decorations from the copper flashing. Cut serpentine strips for the front, making them in one continuous length to fit the area you're covering. Make "sawtooth" strips for the sides. Depending on the length of your flashing, you may need to make these longer sawtooth strips in several pieces to fit the height of the bookcase.

**6**

With the drill and bit, drill small "starter holes" in your copper.

**7**

Lay the bookshelf on its back and hammer the trim onto the front areas of the bookshelf with the copper nails.

**8**

Turn the bookshelf on one side. Starting at the top, hammer the sawtooth trim to the side. If the trim is in several pieces, lap the end of the top strip over the next strip you're laying as you work down from the top to the bottom. Secure this overlap with a nail. Repeat on the other side.

# Chairs

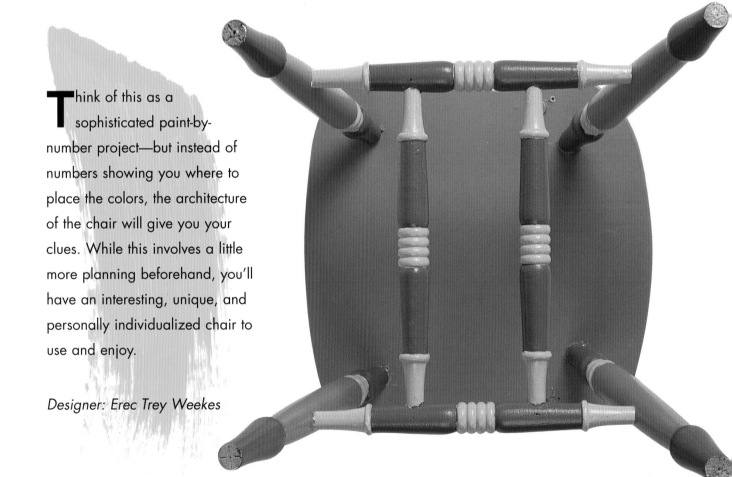

## Painted "Architect-Chair!"

**T**hink of this as a sophisticated paint-by-number project—but instead of numbers showing you where to place the colors, the architecture of the chair will give you your clues. While this involves a little more planning beforehand, you'll have an interesting, unique, and personally individualized chair to use and enjoy.

*Designer: Erec Trey Weekes*

Study the chair before you begin to see where the paint will go. Consider each plane of the chair as a color opportunity. You can paint the back vertical slats alternating colors, one color, or a different color each. The edges of the seat can be a different color from its top, as can the edges of the bowed back from its front and back. The turned legs and rungs on this chair provide logical divisions for applying different colors of paint.

As with any other project, prepare the chair by sanding and priming before beginning to paint. You'll need a 2" (5 cm) angled brush, and may find a 1" (2.5 cm) angled brush helpful for getting into the smaller spaces. Both a flat and round artist's brush can also help with detailing. As for advice, designer Erec Weekes says, "Working on this piece was quite intense and thought provoking—very meditative. All you need is a steady hand and an extra measure of patience."

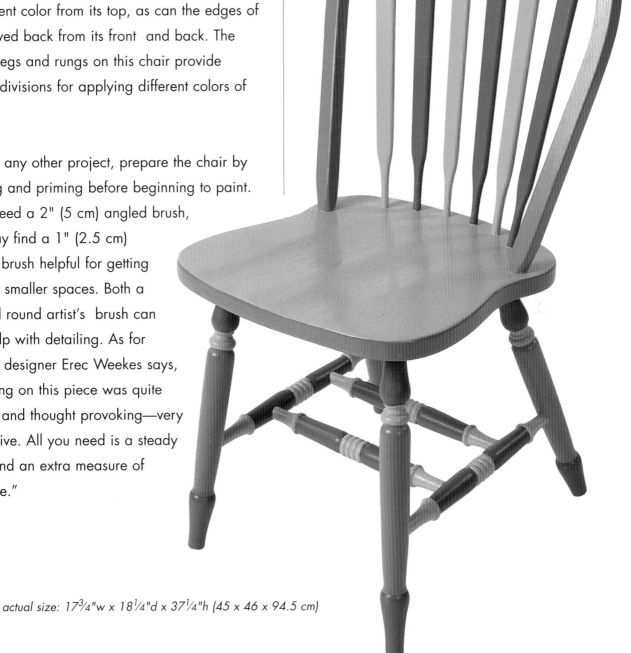

*actual size: 17³/₄"w x 18¹/₄"d x 37¹/₄"h (45 x 46 x 94.5 cm)*

# Children's Rocker

**C**reate an inviting (and fun!) chair for a special youngster in your life. It will become a favorite place for rocking the time away. As a variation, change the colors to brights for a completely different look.

*Designer: Esther P. Doyle*

*actual size: 15"w x 24"d x 27½"h
(38 x 61 x 70 cm)*

## Materials

Child's rocking chair—look for one with many spools on the arms and legs and flat slats on the back.

All-purpose primer

Latex semigloss paint in antique white

Transfer paper

Artist's acrylics in 2-ounce (56-g) jars in light magenta, prism violet, cadmium yellow medium, Hooker's green, blue- green, burnt sienna, burnt umber, and titanium white.

Water-based varnish or polyurethane

## Tools

Extra-fine sandpaper

Tack cloth or damp rag

2½" (6.5 cm) angled brush suitable for latex paint

Artist's acrylic brushes—#8 round, #2 round, and #12 flat.

Toothpicks

Ruler

Pencil

¾" (2 cm) masking tape

*Patterns for this design are on page 138.*

### 1

Using the extra-fine sandpaper, sand the chair until smooth. Wipe off any dust or debris with a tack cloth or damp rag and allow to dry if necessary.

### 2

Prime all surfaces with the all-purpose primer and allow to dry.

### 3

With the 2½" (6.5 cm) brush, apply two coats of the antique white latex paint. Allow the first coat to dry completely before applying the next one. You can quick-dry the first coat with a hair dryer before applying the second coat to shorten your working time. You may want to paint in stages, starting from the bottom, then moving to the top areas once the paint is dry enough to handle. Never paint the very bottom of the rockers since the paint will scuff the floor. Once both coats are applied, allow the chair to dry thoroughly, preferably overnight, before you begin to paint the design.

### 4

Copy the designs on page 000. With the transfer paper or tracing paper, and following the photograph as a visual guide, position, then transfer the flower design onto the backrest of the chair. (See pages 14-15 for transferring instructions.)

### 5

To paint the stems and leaves on the backrest, thin some of the Hooker's green paint with water, use the #12 brush, and paint the stem end toward flower. Load the #8 round artist's brush with Hooker's green, then dip the tip of the brush into the blue-green—this technique is called "double loading" a brush. In each grouping of leaves, use the double-loaded brush to paint the longest leaf first. From leaf end toward the stem, begin by pressing down to fan the brush, then slowly release the pressure to make "comma" strokes near the end to the stem. Follow this same procedure for all the leaves.

**6**

For the daisy, double load the #8 brush, first with yellow, then the tip with light magenta. For each petal, make a comma stroke, ending just inside the oval center.

**7**

Paint the center of the daisy with raw sienna. With the tip end of the #8 brush, or the end of a toothpick, make random dots with white and burnt umber in and around the center. Allow to dry.

**8**

The flowers on the back vertical slats of the chair can be painted freehand, or you can copy the patterns and transfer them to the chair. If you do copy and transfer the design, paint the stems freehand for a more natural look, then place the flowers and leaves over and around the stems.

**9**

With the #2 brush, paint the flowers and stems on the back slats using the same colors as the larger flowers and the same technique of double loading the paint on the brush. Allow to dry.

**10**

Determine how many colors you can alternate on the spools on each side of the chair. If you can alternate three colors, mix a light yellow from equal parts of the cadmium yellow medium and white. Next, mix a lavender from the white and a dot or so of prism violet.

Then, alternate the light magenta with the pale yellow and lavender. If you can't alternate three colors, select two colors from the magenta, light yellow, or lavender to alternate.

**11**

To make the checkerboard seat, first measure to find the center point of the seat. Then use a pencil and ruler to lightly mark the vertical and horizontal axis from this point.

**12**

Using the ¾" (2 cm) masking tape, mask off the checkerboard design. Each row of tape should be spaced exactly ¾" (2 cm) apart. To avoid measuring, just lay rows of tape side by side then remove every other row. Do this both horizontally and vertically. Apply two to three coats of the lavender you mixed in Step 10, allowing each coat to dry completely before applying the next one. Allow all paint to dry, then remove the tape.

**13**

To complete the checkerboard design, use the tape to mask over the lavender areas you painted in Step 12. Then apply two to three coats of the same lavender to the untaped areas, allowing each coat to dry completely before applying the next one. Allow all paint to dry, then remove the tape. To finish, varnish all surfaces with water-based varnish or polyurethane.

# Forest-Camouflage Adirondack Chair and Footrest

**D**epart from the traditional white or weathered finish for your Adirondack chair. Create a haven at wood's edge with this stenciled leaf and fern pattern that can help you become one with your surroundings.

*Designer: Lisa Sanders*

*actual size: chair, 33"w x 38"d x 34½"h  (84 x 96.5 x 87.5 cm)*

## Materials

Adirondack-style chair and footrest

One small can of all-purpose primer

One can forest green spray paint

Assorted leaves

One piece of stencil board or plastic
for making stencil

One piece of cardboard,
slightly bigger than stencil

Artist's acrylic paint, one small tube each in
deep purple and rust red

Latex paint, one small can each in yellow-green,
medium green and forest green

Small plastic bucket for mixing paint

One small can of clear polyurethane

## Tools

Fine-grit sandpaper

Paper or cloth drop cloth

Pencil or fine-point marker

Craft knife

Rubber gloves

One sea sponge

Stir stick

Rags or paper towels

2" or 3" (5 or 7.5 cm) paintbrush

**1**

The following directions apply to the chair and the footrest. For a uniform look, they should be painted together at each step so the colors and the layering are identical.

**2**

Sand both pieces with fine-grit sandpaper, paying special attention to any rough spots. Remove any debris using a damp rag and allow to dry.

**3**

Spread the drop cloth and place the furniture on it. If using primer, paint the furniture with it, allowing it to dry according to the manufacturer's instructions. Note: You do not need to use primer and can directly move on to spray painting the bare wood. However, for a piece that will be used primarily outdoors, an extra coat of primer will provide added protection for the overall life of the piece.

**4**

Apply one coat of green spray paint as the base coat. Start with the underside of the furniture, paying special attention to the spaces between the boards and the crevices. If you don't use a primer, this coat of spray paint and the two final coats of polyurethane will be the only protection these areas receive. Finish spraying on the right side of the furniture, allowing the paint to dry according to the manufacturer's instructions.

**5**

Choose the leaves for stenciling. Lay them one at a time on the stencil board or sheet of plastic stencil material and trace around them with a pencil or marker. Depending on the size of the leaves, draw several leaves on the same piece of stencil material.

**6**

Place the cardboard under the stencil board to create a cushioned cutting surface. Carefully cut out the leaf shapes using the craft knife. Do not cut outside of the leaf outline. Remove the leaf shape, leaving the leaf-shaped hole in the stencil. Follow this procedure with the other leaves.

**7**

Put on the rubber gloves. Using the sea sponge, dab random blotches of dark purple paint on the furniture approximately 24" (61 cm) apart and 4-6" (10-15 cm) across. Rinse out the sponge and repeat, using the rust red paint in other areas. The rust red represents the soil and the purple represents the shadows. Using these together as an undercoat creates a sense of depth.

## 8

When the rust red and purple are dry, use the sea sponge to  apply the forest green paint in random blotches all over the furniture. Repeat using the medium green, and allow to dry.

## 9

Mix equal parts of the yellow-green and the medium green paint, approximately 1 cup (.24 l) each. Place the stencil on the furniture. Using the sponge and the mixed green color, stencil the leaf pattern random-ly over the furniture. Don't forget the edges. You'll get a more natural look if a portion of the leaves (the stencil) extends off the ends and onto the edges. For the bigger leaf shapes, such as maple and oak, sponge the paint unevenly over the stencil, so that the leaf shape will have a shaded look. Allow to dry.

## 10

Repeat the random stenciling with the yellow-green color.  Some of these leaf shapes

should overlap the previous darker green leaf shapes to give it a nice layered effect. Allow paint to dry thoroughly.

## 11

 Using the paintbrush, apply one coat of polyurethane to the entire surface of the furniture. Let dry as recom-mended by manufacturer, then apply a second coat.

# Colorful Kitchen Chairs

**S**ome areas on these chairs have three layers of paint. By sanding those areas when the paint is dry, the colors underneath show through, giving these already colorful chairs extra interest and depth. For this technique, designer Loveeta Baker says, "Oil paint works best." Though it takes more time to dry, she believes it provides a more durable and luminescent finish.

*Designer: Loveeta Baker*

*actual size: 15$\frac{1}{2}$"w x 18$\frac{1}{2}$"d x 34"h*
*(39.5 x 47 x 86.5 cm)*

## Materials

| |
|---|
| Chairs |
| Oil-based stain in a light, natural color |
| Oil-based sealer |
| Oil paint in three colors of your choice |
| Oil-based polyurethane |

## Tools

| |
|---|
| Sandpaper, fine- and medium-grit |
| 2" (5 cm) paintbrushes |
| Masking tape |
| Rags |
| Turpentine |

### 1

Lightly sand the entire chair and remove any debris.

### 2

Following the manufacturer's instructions, apply the stain and allow to dry. Again, following the manufacturer's instructions, apply the sealer and allow to dry.

### 3

Depending on the look you want, you may be using a combination of one, two, or three coats of paint on various parts of the chair. You'll need to think beforehand about the placement of the colors you'll be using to get the effect you want. Most of the sanding, and therefore the layers of paint, on these chairs are on the edges. Once you decide where the paint will go, use masking tape to mask off any areas you want to remain unpainted.

### 4

Apply your first color to the areas that will be sanded and to any other areas that will be that color. Let the paint dry at least 8 hours.

### 5

Mask off the areas that are to remain the first color. Do not mask off the areas that you'll be sanding. Paint the second color over the first on the areas that will be sanded and to any other areas that will be that color. Let the paint dry another 8 hours.

### 6

Mask off the areas that are to remain the first and second color. Do not mask off the areas that you'll be sanding. Paint the final color on the areas to be sanded and on all the remaining areas that will be that color. Allow the paint to dry completely for several days.

### 7

Use the medium-grit sandpaper to sand the areas of the chair that have the layered paint, allowing the colors underneath to show through. Remove any debris.

### 8

Apply a coat of polyurethane to provide a protective finish.

### 9

Clean your brushes well with rags and turpentine.

**TIP:** Make sure your brushes are in good shape and clean before you begin work. Always use a better-quality brush suitable for working with oil paint. If you try to save money with a bargain brush, you'll eventually pay the price in frustration.

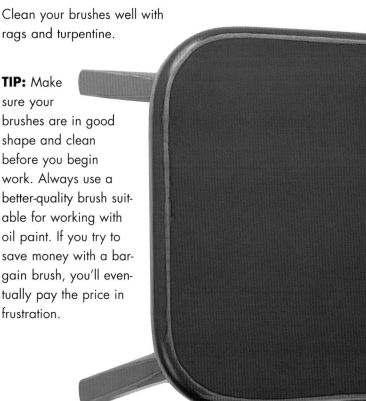

# Stenciled Rocking Chair

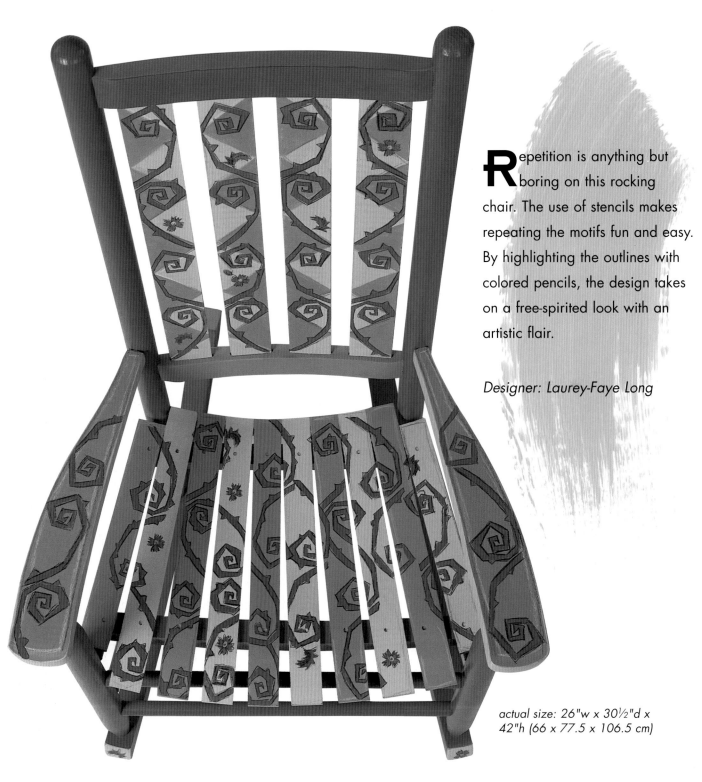

**R**epetition is anything but boring on this rocking chair. The use of stencils makes repeating the motifs fun and easy. By highlighting the outlines with colored pencils, the design takes on a free-spirited look with an artistic flair.

*Designer: Laurey-Faye Long*

*actual size: 26"w x 30½"d x 42"h (66 x 77.5 x 106.5 cm)*

## Materials

| |
|---|
| Rocking chair |
| Acrylic paint in three closely related values of one color— light, medium, and dark |
| Cardstock or manila folder |
| Assorted colored pencils of a good quality |
| Spray acrylic sealer |

## Tools

| |
|---|
| 3" (7.5 cm) paintbrush |
| Ruler |
| Scissors |
| Craft knife |
| Stenciling brush |
| #400 sandpaper |
| Tack cloth or rags |

*Patterns for this design are on page 142.*

Note: Since the stenciling will be done using the darkest color, any area to be stenciled will be painted with the light or medium colors. You may find it helpful to turn the chair upside down and paint from that angle first.

### 1
Apply a base coat of the lightest color to the chair and allow to dry.

### 2
Paint the seat slats, alternating the light and medium colors.

### 3
Paint the back slats with the light color. Allow the paint to dry.

### 4
From the cardstock or manila folder, cut a triangle with a 2" (5 cm) base. Place the 2" (5 cm) base of the triangle at the top left edge of the first back slat. Trace the triangle's outline, then move the triangle down 2" (5 cm) and trace. Repeat this process down the slat.

### 5
When you've finished tracing the triangle all the way down the first slat, flip the triangle over. Place the 2" (5 cm) base of the triangle at the top right edge of the next slat, trace, then move the triangle down before tracing again as in Step 4. Repeat the process of tracing and moving the triangle all the way down the slat. Continue flipping and tracing in this manner on the remaining slats. You'll see the diamond pattern appear.

### 6
Paint every other diamond on the back slats with the medium color. When the paint is dry, use the colored pencils to outline some of the diamonds. Don't try to be neat and tidy when you do this—move the pencil rapidly back and forth to get a fuzzy quality.

### 7
To make the stencils, first copy the patterns for the motifs, then cut them out. Lay these on the cardstock or manila folder, trace around them, then cut the shapes out with a craft knife. Note: The stencil with the large motif will be used on both its "front" and "back" sides to create the symmetrical effect on the chair back. Use a pencil to mark the slats lightly with an "F" or "B" to remind you how to orient the stencil.

### 8
Position the stencil on the first back slat at the location you want it to be and hold it in place. Using the stencil brush and the darkest color, dab the paint over the stencil. Don't load the brush with paint, a slightly dry brush will give the best results. Try to stencil all the "front" areas first, allowing the stencil to dry before flipping it over to stencil the "back" areas. You don't need to be overly concerned with achieving a neat outline.

**9**

Repeat the stenciling process on the seat slats in a more free-form manner. Experiment with placement, use the stencil upside down, slanted, overlaid—any way you want.

**10**

Outline all the stenciled areas with a dark colored pencil. This helps disguise any sloppy outlines and will give the design a more unified and crisp look. You can vary the design by outlining one or two stenciled areas with different colors.

**11**

Randomly place, then stencil the small motifs of the flower and leaf using the stencil brush and darkest color. When dry, outline these with the colored pencils in varying shades of greens and pinks.

**12**

Apply acrylic spray sealer to the entire chair. Do not use a brush-on sealer or varnish, since this may cause the lines made by the colored pencils to run or smear.

**13**

After the sealer has dried, hand sand the stenciled areas with extra-fine #400 sandpaper. Remove any debris with a tack cloth or damp rag, allow to dry if needed, then apply a second coat of sealer.

# Celestial Rocker

**D**esigner Maureen Donahue says, "Be prepared for your visitors to go crazy over this rocker." And just in case they get too comfortable on your front porch and refuse to leave, you can call on the celestial powers to send them home. Then you can spend your time rocking away in heavenly peace.

*Designer: Maureen Donahue*

*actual size: 28"w x 30½"d x 46½"h
(71 x 77.5 x 118 cm)*

## Materials

Rocking chair

Wood filler

¼" (.5 cm) rope

White glue

Masking tape

Optional: Papier-mâché mix, or make your own using wheat paste and newspaper torn into 1½" (4 cm) pieces

Latex paint in blue, light blue, purple, silver, and gold

Trim colors

Twelve ¼ x 1" (.5 x 2.5 cm) wooden dowel pins

Twelve 1" (2.5 cm) wooden balls

Wood glue

Fabric paints

Copy of the sun motif (see page 140)

Cardstock for stencil

Spray glue

Wooden cutouts of moons, suns, and stars, available at craft stores in a variety of sizes

Contact cement

## Tools

Putty knife

Fine- and extra fine-grit sandpaper

2" (5 cm) angled brush

¾" (2 cm) artist's brush

Vise

Drill with ¼" (.5 cm) bit

Craft knife

Cosmetic sponge

Old toothbrush

*The pattern for this design is on page 140.*

**1**

Using the putty knife, fill any imperfections with wood filler, let dry, then sand the patches smooth. Sand the entire chair with fine-grit sandpaper and remove any debris.

**2**

Glue the ¼" (.5 cm) rope around the back and legs of chair. To do this, use the white glue to make a spiral down and around the back and legs. Apply the rope to the glue, using bits of masking tape to hold the rope until the glue dries. To give the rope more texture, you can first cover it with two layers of papier-mâché. To do this, use the papier-mâché mix or make your own following the manufacturer's instructions for mixing wheat paste and using torn pieces of newspaper. (The papier-mâché is not necessary, but adds a little more interest.)

**3**

When the glue dries, paint the chair using the blue, light blue, and silver in different areas. You will need to plan out where you want each color to go before-hand. Try to plan the placement so there will be some variety. Use any indentations or edges to create natural dividing lines. You can leave some areas to be painted with trim colors.

**4**

Paint the raised rope on the back and legs with two coats of silver paint. Sand the chair with extra-fine sandpaper and apply a second coat of the three col-ors. It's best to work from light to dark, so that any errors will be covered by the next color.

**5**

You will need to insert dowels into the balls for attach-ing them to the chair. To do this, place a ball into the

vise. Use the drill and ¼" (.5 cm) bit to make a hole approximately ½" (1.5 cm) deep. Insert a dowel pin with wood glue into the hole. Do this for all the balls, allowing time for the glue to dry. Paint each ball with two coats of trim paint, allowing the paint to dry. Using the fabric paint, dot on colors all over the balls. (If you build up layers of the paint, you can achieve a spike effect.) Let the fabric paint dry at least 24 hours.

**6**

Using the drill and ¼" (.5 cm) bit, drill holes approxi-mately ½" (1.5 cm) deep in the chair at the locations where you want to place the balls. Put wood glue on the end of the dowel that's protruding from one of the painted balls and insert it into a hole in the chair. Repeat for all the balls with dowels.

**7**

Using a copy machine, copy the sun motif, enlarging to the desired size. Use the spray adhesive to mount the copy to the cardstock. With the craft knife, cut out the stencil of the sun.

**8**

Spray the back of the cutout stencil with a light coating of the spray adhesive. Position it on the back of the chair and use the cosmetic sponge to sponge on the gold paint over the stencil. Leave the stencil in place until the paint dries, then apply another coat. When dry, remove the center of the stencil and apply two additional coats of gold paint to the sun's rays and allow to dry.

**9**

Spatter painting will add depth and texture to the paint. Do this by first thinning the silver paint. Next, dip the toothbrush into it, and flick the silver onto the seat and back of the chair.

**10**

Paint all the star, sun, and moon cutouts using silver, gold, and cream-colored paint. When dry, glue these to the rocker using contact cement.

# Lizard Chair

**T**he classic lines of a Queen Anne chair take a surreal twist with this design. The dark outlining makes it look as if the chair's stepped out of an illustration, while the bright fabric and decoupage add an updated, upholstered look. But the real surprise is on the back, where a lounging lizard looks right at home.

*Designer: Maureen Donahue*

*actual size: 25$\frac{1}{2}$"w x 20"d x 41"h (64.5 x 51 x 104 cm)*

## Materials

Chair

Wood filler

$\frac{1}{4}$" (.5 cm) rope

White glue

Masking tape

Modeling clay

Water putty

Wood glue

Black tissue paper

Latex paint in cream, rust, black, and aqua

Trim color paints

Sixteen $\frac{1}{4}$ x 1" (.5 x 2.5 cm) wooden dowel pins

Two 1$\frac{1}{4}$" (3 cm) wooden half balls

Two 1$\frac{1}{4}$" (3 cm) wooden balls

Four 1" (2.5 cm) wooden balls

Four $\frac{3}{4}$" (2 cm) knobs

9" (23 cm) length of a $\frac{3}{4}$" (2 cm) wooden
dowel, cut into 1$\frac{1}{2}$" (4 cm) pieces

Broad-tip permanent marker

30" (76 cm) square piece of
upholstery fabric

Two 8$\frac{1}{2}$ x 11" (21.5 x 28 cm) color copies
of the fabric at a 45% reduction

## Tools

Putty knife

Fine and extra-fine sandpaper

2" (5 cm) angled brush

$\frac{3}{4}$" (2 cm) artist's brush

Large rubber or plastic lizard to use in casting

Craft knife

Vise

Drill with $\frac{1}{4}$" (.5 cm) bit

Comb

Staple gun and staples

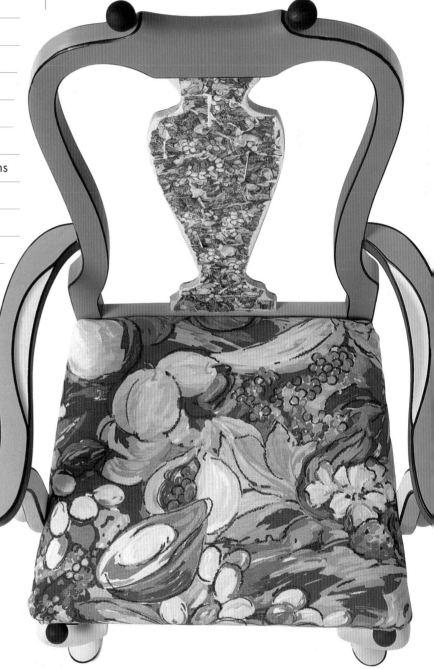

**1**

Remove the seat from the chair. Using the putty knife and wood filler, fill any imperfections in the chair, allow to dry, then sand the patches smooth. Sand the entire chair with the fine-grit sandpaper and remove any debris.

**2**

On the areas below the seat, use white glue to glue the $\frac{1}{4}$" (.5 cm) rope in a random design. To do this, run a line of glue, apply the rope, then tape over the rope with bits of masking tape to hold the rope in place while the glue dries.

**3**

To make the lizard, take the rubber or plastic lizard and apply modeling clay to its back, pressing around it to make a mold. Remove the lizard. Mix the water putty according to the manufacturer's instructions, then pour the putty into the clay mold. Let the putty dry at least three days before removing the clay. Sand any rough or high spots on the putty lizard. Using wood glue, glue it to the back of the chair.

**4**

Using the modeling clay, fill any gaps between the lizard and the chair. Take a sheet of black tissue paper and moisten it with a solution of white glue that has been very diluted with water. Apply it to the lizard, trimming away any excess with a craft knife.

**5**

Paint the chair using the cream, rust, and aqua paints in different areas. You will need to plan where you want each color to go beforehand. Try to plan the placement so there will be some variety. Use the edges to create a natural dividing line.

**6**

When dry, sand with the extra-fine sandpaper, removing any debris, then apply a second coat of the three colors. Work from light to dark, so that any errors will be covered by the darker color.

**7**

Highlight the raised areas on the rope using the trim colors and a dry brush technique. To dry brush, dip the brush into paint that has been slightly thinned. Wipe some of the paint off the brush onto a rag, then brush the paint lightly over the raised areas.

**8**

You will need to insert dowels into the balls for attaching. To do this, place a ball into the vise. Use the drill with a $\frac{1}{4}$" (.5 cm) bit to make a hole approximately $\frac{1}{2}$" (1.5 cm) deep. Insert a dowel pin with wood glue into the hole. Do this for all the balls, allowing the glue to dry, then paint each ball with two coats of trim paint. Note: the $\frac{3}{4}$" (2 cm) balls are actually knobs with a flat side and require no drilling—after painting, glue them directly to the chair using contact cement.

**9**

Using the drill and the $\frac{1}{4}$" (.5 cm) bit, drill holes approximately $\frac{1}{2}$" (1.5 cm) deep in the chair at the locations where you want to place the balls. Put wood glue on the end of the dowel that's protruding from one of the painted balls and insert it into a hole in the chair. Repeat for all the balls with dowels.

**10**

Using a broad-tipped black permanent marker, outline all the "seams" of the chair. For a textured highlight, paint the front of the chair with thinned black paint, then, when the paint is still wet, use the comb to randomly "comb" it off.

**11**

Tear the color copies into smallish pieces. Slightly dilute some white glue with water. Using the artist's brush, apply the glue to the backrest of the chair, then adhere the torn pieces of paper to it.

**12**

To cover the seat of the chair, lay the fabric right-side-down on a clean flat surface, then center the seat right-side-down on top of it. Take one of the edges of fabric and bring it over the side of the seat. Using the staple gun, staple the fabric to the back of the seat at the midway point of the side's measurement. Do the same on the opposite side, stretching the fabric firmly before stapling. Repeat this procedure on the other two sides of the seat. Once the fabric is tacked down at these four points, continue to staple the fabric to the seat, stretching the fabric as you work. To give the upholstery a nice smooth look, apply an even tension as you stretch. Place the seat back on the chair.

# Dining Room Chairs

**T**hese whimsical dining room chairs will delight your family and guests. They show how embellishments can enhance and highlight any painted piece. The use of painted wooden balls, rope, washers, and dowels create a texture that's both unique and handsome.

*Designer: Maureen Donahue*

*actual size: 19"w x 20½"d x 38"h (48.5 x 52 x 96.5 cm)*

## Materials

Chair

Wood Filler

¼" (.5 cm) rope

White glue

Masking tape

¼ x 1" (.5 x 2.5 cm) wooden dowel pins

Washers

Papier-mâché mix (or make your own using wheat paste and  newspaper torn into 1½" (4 cm) pieces

Latex paint in teal, purple, black, and gold

Trim colors

Two 1¼" (3 cm) half balls

Three 1¼" (3 cm) balls

Four 1" (2.5 cm) balls

Four ¾" (2 cm) knobs

Wood glue

Contact cement

Gold paint pen

Fabric paints

## Tools

Putty knife

Sandpaper in fine and extra-fine grit

2" (5 cm) angled brush

¾" (2 cm) artist's brush

Vise

Drill with ¼" (.5 cm) bit

**1**

Using the putty knife, fill any imperfections with wood filler, allow to dry, then sand the patches smooth. Using the fine-grit sandpaper, sand the entire chair.

**2**

On the area below the front of the seat, use white glue to glue the ¼" (.5 cm) rope in a random design.

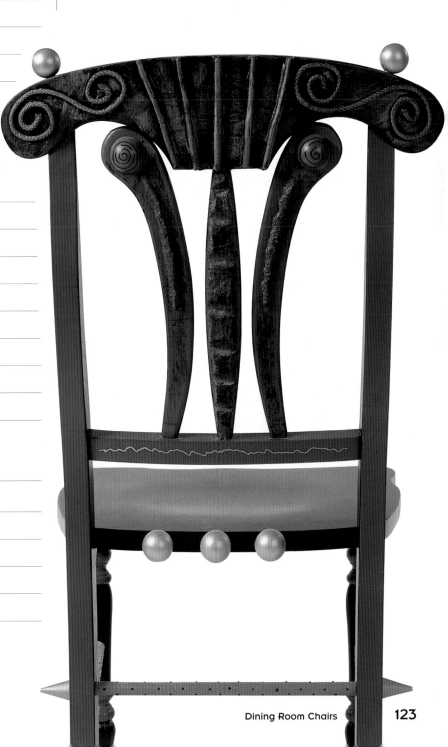

To do this, run a line of glue, apply the rope, then tape over the rope with bits of masking tape to hold the rope in place while the glue dries. On the areas below the sides of the seat, glue dowel pins and washers.

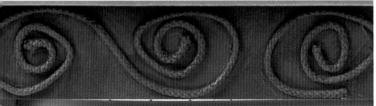

### 3

Make a batch of papier-mâché, either using a mix, or make your own with wheat paste mixed to the manufacturer's instructions and torn newspapers. Form the papier-mâché into a three-dimensional texture or motif of your choice that will fit on the back of the chair, and allow to dry.

### 4

On the back of the chair, glue rope, dowel pins, half balls and the three-dimensional papier-mâché motif. You can cover the dowel pins with two layers of papier-mâché, allowing it to dry before applying the dowels to the back—this isn't critical, but will give the dowel pins a nice texture.

### 5

When all the glue is dry, paint the chair using teal, purple, and black in different areas. Do not paint the edges of the seat. You will need to plan out where you want each color to go beforehand. Try to plan the placement so there will be some variety. Use the indentations on the legs and the edges to create natural dividing lines. You can leave some areas to be painted with trim colors.

### 6

After applying the first coat of the three colors and allowing it to dry, apply two coats of gold paint to the seat edge and allow to dry. Sand the rest of the chair with extra-fine sandpaper and apply a second coat of the three colors. It's best to work from light to

dark, so that any errors will be covered by the next color.

**7**

Highlight the raised areas made by the rope, washers, and dowel pins on the sides of the chair using the trim colors and a dry brush technique. To dry brush, dip the brush into paint that has been slightly thinned. Wipe some of the paint off the brush onto a rag, then brush lightly over the raised areas. The trim colors used here are hot pink over the purple, and teal lightened with white to use over the teal. (Both of these colors also look great over the black.)

**8**

You will need to insert dowels into the balls for attaching them to the chair. To do this, place a ball into the vise. Use the drill with a ¼" (.5 cm) bit to make a hole approximately ½" (1.5 cm) deep. Insert a dowel pin with wood glue into the hole. Do this for all the balls, allowing the glue to dry, then paint each ball with two coats of gold paint. Note: the ¾" (2 cm) balls are actually knobs with a flat side and require no drilling—after painting, glue them directly to the chair using contact cement.

**9**

Using the drill and ¼" (.5 cm) bit, drill holes approximately ½" (1.5 cm) deep in the chair at the locations where you want to place the balls. Put wood glue on the end of the dowel that's protruding from one of the painted balls and insert it into a hole in the chair. Repeat for all the balls with dowels.

**10**

As a final touch, use a gold paint pen and draw random designs to the backrest of the chair. For comfort, you want to keep this area free of any three-dimensional decorations. You can also use fabric paint to apply dots of color to some of the painted trim areas.

# Accessories

## Wall Mirror

**T**he use of an easy mix-it-yourself glaze allows you to get this vibrant layered look. Designer Bess Baird says "Step 7 is a fun one! You can rebrush the glaze as many times as you want and play with the design." The gloss gel used to make the glaze extends the drying time of the paint, allowing you extra time to work—and to have fun.

*Designer: Bess Baird*

*actual size: 36 x 22" (91.5 x 56 cm)*

## Materials

Mirror with wooden frame

White latex primer

White latex paint

Acrylic artist's colors in violet,
blue-green, and red-orange

Gloss gel medium, available in
art- and craft-supply stores

Latex varnish

## Tools

Screwdriver

2" (5 cm) paintbrushes

# 320 sandpaper

Tack cloth

Damp rags

Rubber chisel tip, available in art-supply shops

**1**

Remove the mirror from the frame.

**2**

Using the white primer, paint the frame and let dry.

**3**

Since water-based paint (primer) raises the grain of the wood, lightly sand the surface of the primed frame. Remove any debris using a tack cloth or damp rags.

**4**

Paint the frame with white paint and let dry.

**5**

Mix three glazes of violet, blue-green, and red-orange by combining the gloss gel medium with the acrylic artist's colors.

**6**

Using the glazes, paint the frame. Decide beforehand where you want each color to go on the frame. You may need to draw lines lightly with a pencil as guidelines for painting. Then, take one of the glazes and paint the designated areas for that color. Repeat for the other two glazes until the entire frame is painted. Let dry.

**7**

Cover the entire frame with violet glaze. Immediately wipe off certain areas of the violet glaze with the rubber chisel tip. The design of the previously painted frame will show through. (If you are unable to find a rubber chisel tip, place a clean, unused cap eraser on a pencil, and use the eraser as the chisel tip for removing the paint.) Let dry.

**8**

Varnish, using the latex varnish, and let dry.

**9**

Reassemble mirror.

**TIP:** Remember to wash all tools immediately after use.

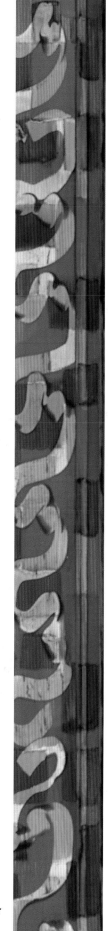

# Rain Forest Coatrack

**L**ooking for something really different? Inspired by the abundant flora and fauna of the rain forest, this coatrack will make you (and your guests) smile every time it's used. You can also adapt this idea to fit your favorite ecosystem.

*Designer: Maureen Donahue*

## Materials

Coatrack

Green latex paint

Black and yellow latex paint

1" (2.5 cm) finishing nails

Rubber or plastic snakes, frogs, bugs, and lizards, four each

Four bunches of silk leaves

## Tools

Fine-grit sandpaper

2" (5 cm) paintbrush, an angled brush works best

Small sponge

Hammer

Glue gun and glue sticks

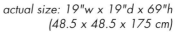

*actual size: 19"w x 19"d x 69"h*
*(48.5 x 48.5 x 175 cm)*

**1**

Sand the coatrack with fine-grit sandpaper. Clean off any debris; then, using the green latex paint, apply the base coat to the coatrack.

**2**

Mix a small amount of the green paint with some black paint to make a darker shade of green. Using the sponge, dip it in the darker green and sponge paint the coatrack by dabbing the color randomly over the green base coat for a mottled effect. Wash out the sponge. After the paint dries, mix a small amount of green with some yellow paint to make a lighter shade of green, and again sponge paint over the base coat and the darker sponged coat.

**3**

Separate the silk leaves from the bunch. Using the glue gun, apply the silk leaves to the base as shown in the photograph. Glue the leaves in layers. That way if the stems aren't very attractive, you can cover them by gluing a leaf over a stem as you work.

**4**

Glue the critters on randomly. If some of the critters are too heavy for the glue, use the hammer and a finishing nail to attach them to the rack.

**5**

Go back to each critter and glue some leaves around and under it. Some of the critters can be tucked under leaves, others can sit on top of leaves.

# Compact Disc Holder

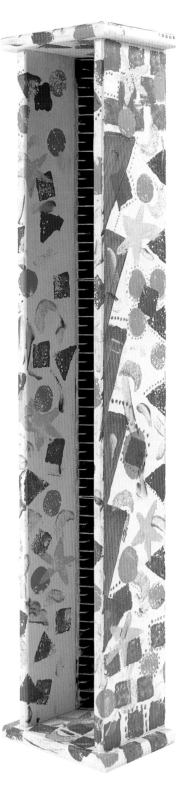

**J**azzy doesn't just refer to music with this colorful CD holder. Sponge-printed shapes in striking colors, combined with hints of glitter, make a sparkling and energetic grace note for brightening your music corner.

*Designer: Nancy McGaha*

## Materials

CD holder

Latex flat paint in off-white

Acrylic craft paint in teal, blue, plum, gold, and silver

Glitter pens in gold, silver, and colors of your choice

## Tools

Three household sponges

Scissors

Craft knife

Paper clips

Disposable styrofoam plates

*actual size: 16"w x 5"d x 26¼"h*
*(40.5 x 12.5 x 66.5 cm)*

**1**

Apply a base coat of the off-white paint to the wood surfaces of the holder and allow to dry.

**2**

While the base coat is drying, draw shapes of your choice on the sponges (used here—star, crescent, square, circle, triangle). You'll find that if you moisten a sponge with water before cutting it, the shapes you cut will hold more paint. Use a scissors or craft knife to cut out the shapes.

**4**

To sponge print, pour some paint onto a small styrofoam plate. Dip the sponge shape into the paint. When it has absorbed enough paint, wipe the excess paint on the side of the plate and apply the sponge to the painted surface of the CD holder.

**5**

Either following a predetermined pattern or creating a random design, sponge print your design to create the effect you want. Use all colors and shapes as desired.

**6**

When the paint is dry, use glitter paints in different colors to add color and glitz. You can create a dotted pattern by gently touching the glitter to the CD holder's surface. For another effect, you can apply the glitter, then smear it onto the surface with your finger. Have fun experimenting with different techniques to create your own unique designs!

# Gilded Mosaic Wall Shelf

**A**dd the glimmer of gold and silver to any room with this small wall unit. By applying metallic leaf (it's easier than you think!) you can quickly transform this plain piece into a prized display for treasured photos or mementos.

*Designer: Kevin Fulford*

*actual size: 8¼"w x 6"d x 39"h (21 x 15 x 99 cm)*

## Materials

| |
|---|
| Wall shelf |
| Latex paint in forest green |
| Water-based leaf size (adhesive) |
| Metallic composition leaf in gold and silver |
| Paste wax |
| Mineral spirits |
| Clear spray acrylic or acrylic varnish |

## Tools

| |
|---|
| 2" (5 cm) disposable foam brush |
| 1" (2.5 cm) bristle brush |
| Rags |
| Spray bottle suitable for holding oil-based products |
| #400 sandpaper |

**1**

Paint the shelf with a base coat of forest green and allow the paint to dry. You can use any color of your choice for the base coat. Note that the leafed surface will be distressed, and this color will show through in places on the finished piece. Any dark color that complements the gold is recommended.

**2**

Since you'll be working one section at a time, mentally divide the piece into sections, such as the back, the shelves, the front, and the top. Beginning with one of these sections, apply the water-based size to that area of the piece. Allow the size to dry slightly until it is tacky to the touch before applying the leaf—never apply leaf to wet size.

**3**

Starting with the silver leaf, tear it into pieces and place on the sized area, working from bottom to top. Next, lay sheets of the gold leaf over the silver leaf and onto the sized areas not covered by the silver.

**4**

Using a stiff-bristle brush, burnish (brush with pressure) the surface. This will remove the excess gold leaf, allowing the silver to show through. Continue burnishing until all remaining leaf fragments are removed from the surface. Do not be concerned with little cracks and lines on

the surface of the leaf—these "faults" add interest to the look of a leafed piece.

**5**

To distress the leafed finish, apply paste wax with a clean rag to those areas of the piece that you want distressed, then buff the wax.

**6**

Slightly thin a small amount of the leaf size with water. Pour the mineral spirits in a spray bottle suitable for holding oil-based products.

**7**

Apply the thinned size to the areas to be distressed, then spritz (spray lightly) with mineral spirits. The size should bead up, giving the surface added texture. Allow to dry.

**8**

When dry, apply another coat of thinned water-based size to the distressed areas. Allow the size to dry slightly until it's tacky to the touch, and apply the gold leaf. Burnish the leaf with the stiff-bristled brush.

**9**

With #400 sandpaper, lightly sand all the areas you distressed. Remove some of the gold leaf down to the paint, allowing the base color to show through. Remove any debris from the surface.

**10**

Either spray with clear acrylic, or apply acrylic varnish with a brush.

# Country French Blue-Rose Shelf

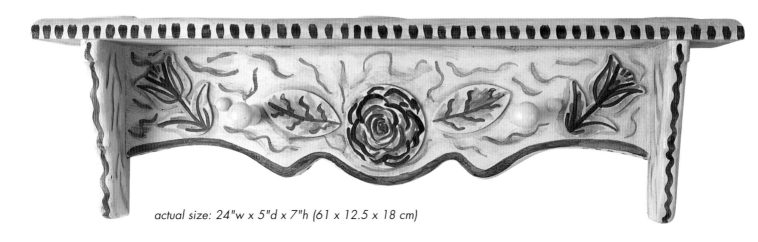

*actual size: 24"w x 5"d x 7"h (61 x 12.5 x 18 cm)*

**T**his charming shelf, washed in blues, will add a fresh look to any room. It's a unique way to use wooden appliques in a whole new way.

*Designer: Anne McCloskey*

## Materials

Wooden shelf with curved lines and pegs

Acrylic matte varnish

Wooden appliqués in sizes to fit your shelf, 11 leaves, 1 round, and 2 flowers—these thin, flat shapes are available at craft stores or you can make your own

Acrylic craft paints in white, dark blue, and medium blue

Colored chalk

White craft glue

Sawtooth hook

## Tools

Fine-grit sandpaper

Tack cloth or dampened paper towel

2" (5 cm) disposable foam brush

Two artist's brushes, one small and round, one small and flat

Hammer

**1**

Using the fine-grit sandpaper, lightly sand the entire shelf, removing any bumps or rough areas. Using a tack cloth or damp paper towel, remove any debris. Allow to dry if necessary.

**2**

Using the foam brush, coat all surfaces of the shelf generously with varnish and allow to dry. Varnish the wooden appliqués on their fronts and sides, and allow to dry.

**3**

Apply two coats of white acrylic paint to the shelf and to the wooden appliqués (on their fronts and sides). Allow the first coat to dry completely before applying the second one.

**4**

You'll paint the appliqués in a free-form manner using several shades of blue wash and the round brush. To paint the rose, begin by thinning the dark blue paint slightly with water. Starting in the middle of the round appliqué, paint small, tight C-strokes (a paint stroke that resembles a C shape) around the shape and out toward the edges. You want to fill the appliqué with the strokes but you don't want to cover the white completely. Allow to dry.

**5**

To get the soft watercolor look, mix a wash of blue by adding water to the dark blue paint. You may want to experiment on paper first to see how light you would like the wash to be, since adding more water makes a lighter wash. You can also make and use several shades of wash, since this will add more interest and enhance the overall look.

**6**

Paint the wash around each of the C-strokes, being careful not to completely cover all the white background. Use this same paint and wash technique on all the wood shapes.

**7**

To paint the flower appliqués, follow the shape of the flower as a guide for painting a simple flower design, allow to dry, then wash around it and allow to dry.

**8**

For the 11 leaves, paint the central vein using a straight line, then add squiggly lines to each side of it. Allow to dry. Paint your wash along the vein lines and allow to dry.

**9**

Using the white craft glue, glue each shape one at a time. First, center the rose at the middle of the shelf front. Next, place leaves on each side of the rose. Then affix the flowers to the far right and left of the front of the shelf. If you need guidelines to help you in placing the appliqués, use chalk for making the marks, then wipe the chalk away once the appliqués are glued in place.

**10**

Glue one leaf to each side of the shelf. Scatter the remaining leaves on the top of the shelf and glue.

Front of shelf

Top

## 11

Allow the glue to dry completely. Using a light blue wash, paint around each appliqué and allow to dry.

## 12

Using the flat brush and the dark blue paint, paint a squiggly line down each of the front-facing side edges of the shelf.

## 13

Again, using the flat brush, paint a broad stroke that follows the curve of the bottom front. At the top, make rectangular slashes, starting from the left back and going all around to right back. Don't worry if the brush strokes aren't perfect—you want them to be loose and free-flowing to achieve the country look.

## 14

Starting at the top with the medium blue paint, paint a series of curvy lines around the shapes. As quickly as you paint a line, wash your brush out in water, blot most of the water out on a paper towel, then stroke over the curvy line. This will purposely blur the line and give it a very soft look. Allow this section to dry. Repeat making the curvy blurred lines around the shapes on one section of the shelf at a time. To prevent runs, always allow the paint to dry before moving to the next section. When all sections are painted, allow the shelf to dry completely.

## 15

Apply a coat of varnish and allow to dry. If needed for extra protection, apply a second coat of varnish.

## 16

Using the hammer, attach the sawtooth hook to the back of the shelf for hanging.

# Bird Coatrack

The inspiration for this coatrack came from the imported painted bird which designer Mary Devereaux found in a local shop. "The bird's expression and colors pleased me. I selected colors to match the bird's body, down to the red feet of the rack to correspond with the bird's talons."

*Designer: Mary Devereaux*

## Materials

Coatrack

Ornament

Semigloss acrylic paints in colors to match the ornament (used here—hot magenta, apricot, and red)

Permanent paint markers in opaque colors to match the ornament (used here—pink, yellow, and orange

One screw

Clear acrylic household adhesive

## Tools

Mixing container—an old jar works best

2" (5 cm) disposable foam brushes

½" (1.5 cm) flat artist's brush

Rags or paper towels

Jigsaw

Small hand or power drill

Because your ornament may be different, follow these general procedures for creating your own design.

## 1

The bird's main body color is hot magenta, while its second most prominent color is apricot. Since these two colors vibrate playfully together to create a warm peach, this color became the third color of the design. To get this color, mix ⅔ magenta paint to ⅓ apricot.

## 2

Start painting at the top with the magenta, continuing until you're about ⅓ down the length of the rack. While the magenta is still wet, take a clean brush and paint the warm peach color mixed in Step 1 approximately ⅔ of the way down the rack. Where the magenta and peach meet, blend them together by "feathering." To do this, keep your foam brush almost dry—you may want to keep an absorbent cloth handy for dabbing excess paint off the brush—then lightly brush the two colors together using long blending strokes.

## 3

Where the peach color ends, and while that paint is still wet, take the apricot color and paint the rest of the way down, stopping at the top of the feet. Use the same feathering/dry-brush technique to blend the peach and apricot colors. Allow the paints to dry. Note: When you're working on this section of the rack, you want to work rapidly before the paints dry so you can properly blend the colors together.

## 4

Following the feathering/dry-brush technique described in Steps 2 and 3, paint the legs of the rack. Paint one leg at a time, blending pure magenta into red.

## 5

To make the dots which imitate the bird's plumage, use the markers in a completely random stipple pattern after the paint is completely dry. The dots add to the whimsy of the piece, echoing the bird's style, and they also help the eye make the transition between blended colors.

## 6

Use the ½" (1.5 cm) flat artist's brush to detail the separations where the legs and hooks meet the body of the rack, and for the button-shaped hardware.

## 7

Depending on the ornament you'll be using, you may want to create a platform for it to better secure it to the rack. To do this, use a jigsaw and cut a scrap from ¼" (.5 cm) plywood, or from other thin sheets of wood, in a shape that approximately fits the base of the ornament. Once cut, paint the base and allow to dry.

## 8

Drill a hole through the base, then drill a corresponding hole in the coatrack. Attach the base to the rack with a screw. Use the glue to adhere the ornament to the base.

**TIP:** Other ideas for ornaments that may inspire you:
- a papier-mâché vegetable or fruit
- one-of-a-kind ceramic or clay sculpture
- a geometric shape of glass or metal
- whatever matches the mood of your coats and the theme of the room where the rack will reside.

*actual size:*
*19"w x 19"d x 67"h*
*(48.5 x 48.5 x 170 cm)*

# Patterns

Enlarge to desired size.

These patterns are for the project on page 46, Painted Floral Table.

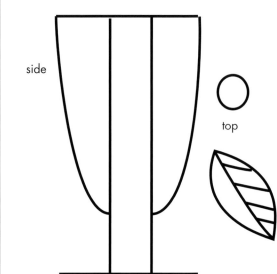

side

top

These patterns are for the project on page 28, Children's Table and Chairs.

Table legs

yellow

white

white

white

Tabletop

yellow

orange

yellow

orange

Underside of tabletop

yellow

yellow

orange

orange

yellow

red or royal blue

Underside of tabletop

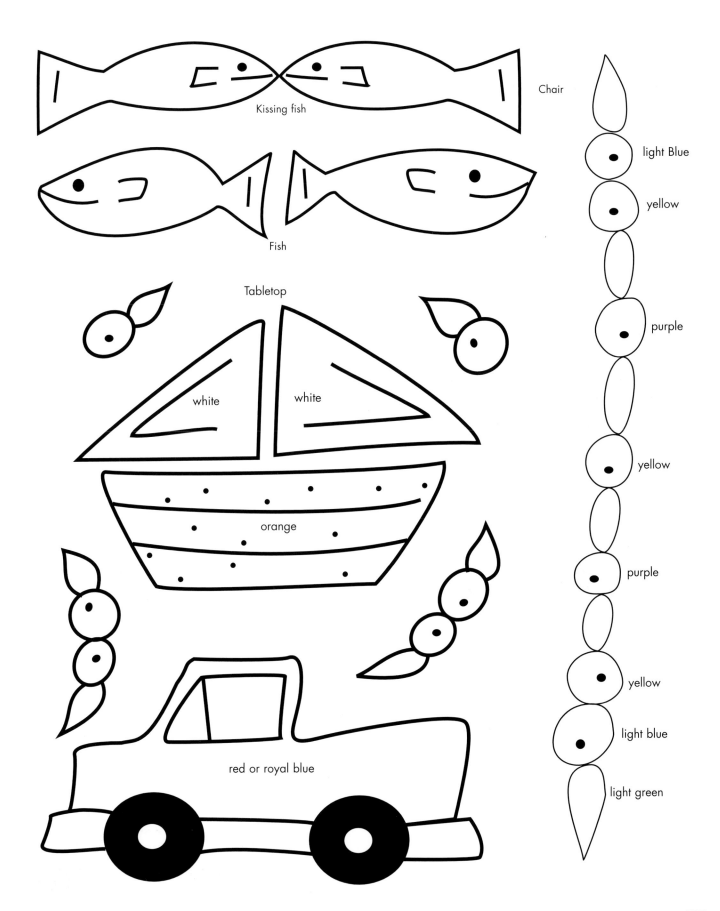

Kissing fish

Chair

Fish

Tabletop

white

white

orange

red or royal blue

light Blue

yellow

purple

yellow

purple

yellow

light blue

light green

These patterns are for the project on page 52,
Trompe L'Oeil Teatime Table.

These patterns are for the project on page 104,
Children's Rocking Chair.

These patterns are for the project on page 69,
Optical Illusion Three-Drawer Chest.

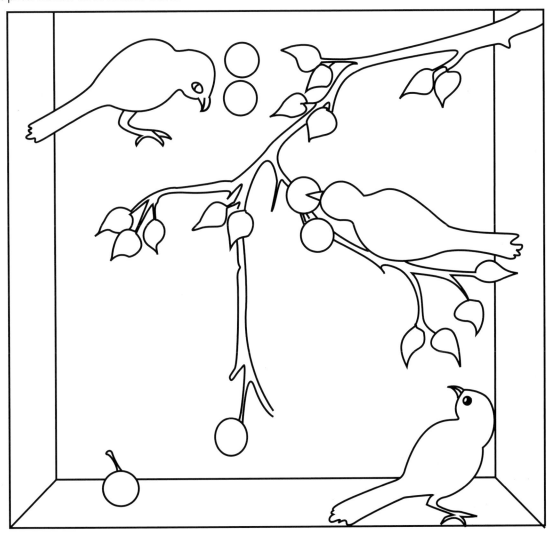

Place on the right side at
the bottom front corner.

Place on the top at the
left front corner.

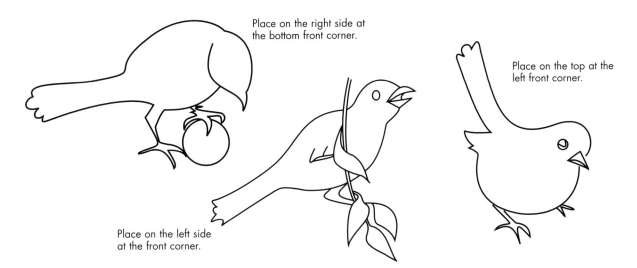

Place on the left side
at the front corner.

These patterns are for the project on page 80, Flowered Bar Stool.

Small flower for legs

pink

Large flower for top

light blue

light green

light green

yellow

pink

Legs

light green

light blue

light green

This pattern is for the project on page 115, Celestial Rocker.

These patterns are for the project on page 88, Weathered Fish Bench.

Fish for side legs

Big fish for top

Small fish for cross bar

This pattern is for the project on page 25, Frog Table.

These patterns are for the project on page 112, Steciled Rocking Chair.

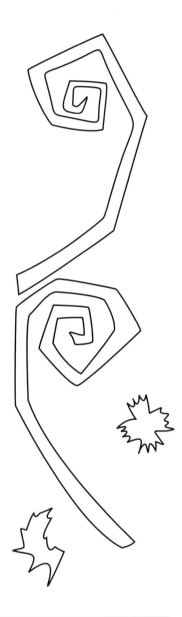

These patterns are for the project on page 92, Tropical Whimsey Bookcase.

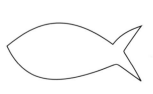

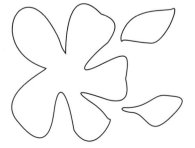

## Contributing Designers

**Bess Baird**, a mural artist who also enjoys sculpting and gilding, is a graduate of the City & Guilds of London Decorative Arts and Restoration Program in Asheville, North Carolina. Her lush, bright colors and sense of fun mirror her effervescent outlook on life.

**Loveeta Baker**, a freelance textile designer and artist, is taking a break from the nine-to-five world to work on a variety of creative projects including textile print design, collage, and sculpture.

**Deborah Cavenaugh**, from Wilmington, North Carolina, is a fine artist who wonderfully translates her brilliant color sense and detailed designs to the three-dimensional world of painted furniture.

**Mary Devereaux** is a currently conducting a research project about adolescents through Duke Medical Center. Her creative pursuits, however, keep her constantly in touch with the artistic realm through her jewelry design, photography, watercolor, freelance graphics, and fashion design. Her e-mail address is Odever@aol.com.

**Maureen Donahue (Cha Cha)**, a graphic artist, lives with her five cats in Asheville, North Carolina. She is a multi-talented designer who enjoys experimenting in different mediums to produce one-of-a-kind items which she sells through national wholesale craft markets. In her free time, she enjoys riding her Harley Davidson motorcycle through the beautiful mountains of North Carolina.

**Esther Doyle**, from Charlotte, North Carolina, has spent more than 20 years in critical care nursing but has been working at her artistic avocation for more than 40 years. She enjoys using lively colors to produce artistic furniture with traditional appeal. She sells her work under her business name *Highlander Folk* and can be reached by e-mail at HighlanderFolk@compuserv.com.

**Lyna Farkas** is a teacher, consultant, and artisan in decorative painting and restoration. Through her business, *In the Spirit of Decorum*, located in Asheville, North Carolina, she uses her many talents to create personalized decorative textures for her clients whether on floor cloths, furniture, or structures.

**Kevin Fulford** is a professional decorative painter who works with interior designers on residential sites and in creating interior showrooms. He is a graduate of the City & Guilds of London Advanced Decorative Painting and Restoration Program. He has worked in High Point, North Carolina, for internationally known furniture manufacturers and designers.

**Gay Grimsley**, has her own business creating and selling one-of-a-kind painted and gilded furniture and accessories. She specializes in custom faux finishes and stenciling.

**Laurey-Faye Long**, with her husband Steven Tengelsen, are co-owners of *Ruby Dog Wood*, a woodworking business in the mountains of Western North Carolina. Together they build and paint wood furniture and accessories. They devote their spare time to completing their hand-built home, gardening, and their hound-dog Ruby.

**Shelly Lowell** is a graphic designer, illustrator, and fine artist. Originally from New York City, she graduated from Pratt Institute with a BFA in Advertising and Visual Communications. She has received many national awards and her work has been exhibited in museums and galleries in New York, Atlanta, and San Francisco. Her work is in private and corporate collections.

**Nancy Taylor McGaha** enjoys mixing media and craft techniques. She works in a variety of crafts, particularly bead-work—both loomed and peyote stitch, rigid-heddle loom weaving, smocking, and fiber-art wall hangings.

**Anne McCloskey** is a member of the national Society of Craft Designers. She has written a craft column, designed crafts for leading magazines, books, trade shows, and television programs. She enjoys experimenting with new materials in order to create original, whimsical, and trendy projects.

**Lindsey Morgan** of Hendersonville, North Carolina, is a decorative painter. A graduate of the City & Guilds of London Decorative Arts and Restoration Program, she currently works on selected projects between her studies as a full-time student.

**Molly Tilden Rousey**, with a background in visual arts and technical theater, is a busy decorative artist who produces custom hand-painted floor cloths and furniture. Specializing in bright colors and playful themes, her work is currently exhibited and sold in Wilmington, North Carolina. As a mother with young children, she enjoys being able to pursue her art and manage her business from her home.

**Lisa Sanders** has designed lingerie for 14 years for major brand names. She has travelled all over the world and is currently a freelance designer working in apparel, home furnishings, and crafts. She enjoys exploring different techniques and translates her sense of design from one medium to another with ease.

**Traci Dee Neil-Taylor** is a freelance photographer with an interest in multimedia art. She owns *The Cellar* in Asheville, North Carolina, which sells a large variety of gifts and provides darkroom rental for film development.

**Erec Trey Weekes** is an artist who creates murals, commissioned pieces, and painted furniture through his business *Art for All Seasons*. He enjoys transforming everyday objects into inviting works of art. He believes that creating a mood for a piece, both through imagery and the music he listens to as he works, infuses it with a magic all its own.

**Ellen Zahorec** lives in Cincinnati, Ohio, where she is a mixed-media artist specializing in handmade paper and collage. Her work has been shown internationally and is part of numerous private and corporate collections.

## Acknowledgments

Special thanks to Marshall Manche, owner of Wood You Furniture in Asheville, North Carolina, for providing designer support, and for allowing us to use his store for photography. To all the talented designers, for their enthusiastic response to this project and for their incredible creative gifts. To Celia Naranjo, art director, for her insight, encouragement, and especially for her strength. To Evan Bracken, photographer, for his good counsel and artistic eye. To Hannes Charen, art production, for his sense of humor and patience.

Most of the pieces featured in this book were obtained from Wood You Furniture. Since 1977, Wood You Furniture has been selling quality unfinished real-wood furniture for less. Wood You has more than 30 locations to serve you. For the location nearest you, contact them at: www.woodyoufurniture.com.

## Index